William Elliot Griffis

The Romance of Conquest

The story of American expansion through arms and diplomacy

William Elliot Griffis

The Romance of Conquest
The story of American expansion through arms and diplomacy

ISBN/EAN: 9783337065843

Printed in Europe, USA, Canada, Australia, Japan

Cover: Foto ©ninafisch / pixelio.de

More available books at **www.hansebooks.com**

THE
ROMANCE OF CONQUEST

*THE STORY OF AMERICAN EXPANSION
THROUGH ARMS AND DIPLOMACY*

BY

WILLIAM ELLIOT GRIFFIS
MEMBER OF THE AMERICAN HISTORICAL ASSOCIATION
AUTHOR OF "BRAVE LITTLE HOLLAND," "THE PILGRIMS IN THEIR
THREE HOMES," "THE ROMANCE OF DISCOVERY," "THE
ROMANCE OF AMERICAN COLONIZATION," ETC.

ILLUSTRATED BY

FRANK T. MERRILL

BOSTON AND CHICAGO
W. A. WILDE COMPANY

Copyright, 1899,
By W. A. Wilde Company
All rights reserved.

THE ROMANCE OF CONQUEST.

TWO COPIES RECEIVED,

Dedicated to
MY COMRADES
IN THE FORTY-FOURTH PENNSYLVANIA VOLUNTEERS

(MERCHANTS' REGIMENT OF PHILADELPHIA)

WHO HAD AND WHO HAVE

FAITH IN GOD AND THEIR COUNTRY

PREFACE.

When the "Free Quakers" of Philadelphia inscribed on their new meeting-house "Erected in the year of our Lord, 1783, of the Empire 8," they were not "Jingos" or "imperialists," but believers in God and in the growth of the United States of America. Among these Friends, who had drawn sword for their country, were my ancestors and kinsmen. It is not wonderful that their descendant inherits also their view.

To-day there are those who read the words "empire" and "expansion" in the same light. They see in the events of the pivotal year of 1898 the Divine hand, and they hear in the new developments fresh calls to duty. On history is based surest prophecy. Those who are most familiar with the story of our country will be best fitted to comprehend intelligently the part they are called upon to play in the future.

With emphasis upon the original meaning of the word "conquest," I have in this volume told the story of our national expansion and of the triumphs of American arms and diplomacy from July 4, 1776, when we began to be a corporate nation or empire, until this first year of Greater America.

Expansion, either of ideas or of territory, is no new thing to Americans. The Northwest Territory, the Louisiana Purchase, the acquisitions of Florida, Texas, Oregon, California, the Gadsden Purchase, and Alaska were but the preludes to the annexation of Hawaii and of island territory in the Indies, both East and West.

The story is one without partisanship. Those who built the Greater America were not Federalists or Whigs, Democrats or Republicans, but patriots. The brave soldiers who defended the flag in the field, the sailors who bore it in peace or war to the ends of the earth, the diplomatists abroad or the statesmen at home, were of all parties. In forming our national policy they represented no section, but the nation only. To do justice to all the makers of Greater America, of every race and color, has been my aim. If in this work I have given more prominence to the navy than the average historical writer, it is because the facts require it. Indeed, it is only now that our people seem waking up to the full importance of our marine and its influence upon the development of the greatest, as it will be, we trust, the best, nation on earth.

W. E. G.

ITHACA, N.Y.,
April, 1899.

TABLE OF CONTENTS.

CHAPTER		PAGE
I.	Westward the Course of Empire	13
II.	From Lexington to Stillwater	22
III.	The Navy in the Revolutionary War	31
IV.	From Saratoga to Yorktown	39
V.	The Stars and Stripes in the Mediterranean	47
VI.	From Confederation to Constitution	57
VII.	The Movement beyond the Alleghanies	66
VIII.	War with France on the Sea	76
IX.	Our Navy in the Mediterranean	86
X.	Doubling the National Domain	97
XI.	Why a Second War for Freedom was Fought	104
XII.	The Naval Campaign of 1812	113
XIII.	Our Flag kept Flying on Lakes and Seas	120
XIV.	"Old Ironsides" and Cotton Bales	129
XV.	Madison and Monroe	140
XVI.	The Seminole and Black Hawk Wars	149
XVII.	Our Northwestern Empire	162
XVIII.	Old "Rough and Ready" in Mexico	175
XIX.	The Navy and Army at Vera Cruz	189
XX.	Scott's Advance to the City of Mexico	200
XXI.	The American Sailor in the Far East	213

CHAPTER		PAGE
XXII.	CONFEDERATES AND FEDERALS	221
XXIII.	THE WAR FOR FREEDOM	233
XXIV.	A UNITED COUNTRY	244
XXV.	AMERICAN MARINES AND SAILORS IN KOREA	251
XXVI.	OUR EXPANDING EMPIRE ON THE PACIFIC	263
XXVII.	OUR WAR WITH SPAIN	275
XXVIII.	THE AMERICAN FLAG IN THE PHILIPPINES	284
XXIX.	SANTIAGO AND PORTO RICO	290
XXX.	THE GREATER UNITED STATES	299

ILLUSTRATIONS.

		PAGE
The Continental Soldier . . *Frontispiece*		23
"Why do you do that?" said the President .		61
The Battle of New Orleans		136
Captain May's Charge at Resaca de la Palma		178
March to the Sea .		241

THE ROMANCE OF CONQUEST.

CHAPTER I.

WESTWARD THE COURSE OF EMPIRE.

BETWEEN the ideas of discovery and conquest there is a close connection, for most nations that have made discoveries proceeded to conquer and subdue the new-found lands. Yet not all nations succeed in planting colonies. The Spanish, French, and Portuguese failed. As Powers, they have passed out of America. The two modern peoples who have best succeeded are the English and the Dutch. These now lead the way with precedents and experience. The people that are now leaving the limits of their continent and entering upon this part of the world's work, in both the Indies, are the Americans.

Although their own first home land was only the Atlantic coast strip between the ocean and the Alleghanies, yet they have won by discovery, colonization, arms, or diplomacy the whole region bounded by the Atlantic and the Pacific and the northern lakes and the Gulf; the vast territory of Alaska, inland and insular; and large possessions in the East and the West Indies. The United States of America have become, in the full sense of the word, a World Power, and, in a double sense, "the great Pacific Power."

The expansive movement of human history was first from Mesopotamia to the Mediterranean, then to the Atlantic, then to the Pacific Ocean, and it is still onward. The Far East has become the Near West.

There have been many kinds of conquest, some by deliberate plan long before thought out, and again by sudden action on account of necessity. Some were in righteousness; others in wrong and cruelty. In this book we shall write the romance of American conquest, which began in colonial days. Though at times marked with wrong and injustice, as all human history is, in the main it is a story of honorable acquisition.

What is a conqueror, and what is conquest? One thinks of the word, which sounds so grand in poetry, as in Mrs. Hemans's verse:—

> "Bring flowers to strew in the conqueror's path,
> He hath shaken thrones with his stormy wrath;
> The turf looked red where he won the day.
> Bring flowers to strew in the conqueror's way."

With conquest we associate the idea of subjugation. Now it is well to look at the meaning of words, and note how they change. Let us see how the term "conqueror" grew into its present shape.

Back in the old Roman days the treasurer, commissary, or quartermaster was called a quæstor. To this day the treasurers in the Dutch churches in Holland and America are called quæstors. Then a con-quæstor, or conquisitor, was a man who searched for, and procured, brought together and collected, money, men, or supplies. In other words, he was a recruiting officer. Out of this old Latin mother-word came ours. So also a "conqueror" in the Middle Ages, even when applied to William of Normandy, did not mean one who unlawfully seized land or possessions or subjugated a nation, but rather one who purchased or acquired territory. In old feudal law "conquest" meant the acquisition of property by other means than by inheritance. In Scotch law "conquest" still refers to property acquired by purchase, or gift, or by marriage contract.

American conquest has never meant forcible seizure or cruel treatment. In old days when the Roman armies won victory over their enemies they subjugated them. This means that they put them under the yoke, like beasts of burden. When the people were too many to place a literal yoke on their necks, two spears were set into the ground and to these uprights a third spear was held or tied crosswise. Then all the defeated, men, women, and children, had to bow their heads and pass under in token of submission. In the ancient days conquest was often accompanied with cruelty, torture, and mutilation. Thousands were torn from their homes and settled as colonies of prisoners in other lands. One has only to look at the Assyrian sculptures to see how captives had their eyes put out or their limbs chopped off, or were driven in chains like wild beasts to hard labor and slavery. In Rome, war-captives were used as prey for the lions in the arena, or as gladiators who fought and killed each other to amuse the crowd on a holiday.

No such story is that of American conquest. First of all, we must have righteousness on our side.

"Then conquer we must
When our cause it is just,"

is in our national song. Ours is indeed a brilliant record of conquest through valor and diplomacy, but unaccompanied by the atrocities of ancient or mediæval warfare. Furthermore, the American idea of conquest means moral responsibility, gifts to the conquered of the best that the conquerors can bestow, the blessings of peace, plenty, equal rights, just laws, education, and such participation in social and political rights as may be possible.

In reality, ours has always been a discovering, a colonizing, and a conquering nation from the moment of its birth. Our fathers had first to gain their own freedom and then to defend not only their own frontiers, but to send out expeditions beyond, to win their way against hostile Indians, or against other claimants of land which the States considered their own. In reality, we bought our way, paying for what we got. France, Spain, Great Britain, Russia, Mexico, were all given money, or a full equivalent, for what we got from them.

The United States also sent out exploring expeditions to find new lands, to unveil coast lines, and make the world better known to its inhabitants. Liberia was established in Africa. Commodore Wilkes revealed to the nations an Antarctic continent. Our brave sailors have gone near to the north pole. In many Asiatic and African countries and in the islands of the Pacific, American missionaries and teachers went out in numbers exceeding those of regiments. These, as well as our merchants and mariners, have carried the name and fame of America abroad. Nothing can restrain the pushing ardor of the Anglo-Saxon, who believes that God formed the earth to be inhabited.

After the Civil War and consolidation, peace came, a double duty was put upon the nation of first pacifying and then educating the redmen, and of raising up the black citizens to the appreciation of their rights. With all our faults and shortcomings as a nation, we have honestly striven to do this.

The spirit of American conquest—using the word in the old meaning—was incarnated in George Washington. He was, in a twofold sense, a surveyor of land and of nations. Washington, the engineer and statesman, educated mainly outdoors and among men, was far-sighted enough to see that on this continent the old Latin ideas were to give way before Anglo-Saxon ideas and institutions. As a true Englishman and Virginian, he was glad to lead a company into Pennsylvania and Ohio to dispute the claims of the French, which he believed were not righteously founded.

During the Revolutionary War, when Indians became hostile foreigners, Washington despatched General Sullivan into what was then, 1779, "the Far West" of New York, to assert American claims against the Six Iroquois Nations. During his presidency, he sent Generals St. Clair and Wayne to maintain our rights against the British and redmen in the Northwest. He himself personally visited the waterways and roads of western New York and Virginia, paying great attention to the opening and development of the West. He quickly discriminated between Anglo-Saxon ideas, represented by Great Britain, even when her king was

foolish and hot-headed and Parliament was wrong,
as against the French, who, like the Spanish, Portuguese, and Italians, represented Latin notions, which
were behind the age, and therefore unworkable in
the New World. He taught "Citizen Genet" and
the world a lesson, while also showing Americans
that they must be neither French nor English, but
throw off the colonial spirit of dependence and
become American.

Then, as his latest and best gift to the American
people he issued his farewell address, now a classic.
In this he pointed out that the interests of Europe
or the Mediterranean nations were not ours, and
that we had problems of our own. We had nothing to do with their scheme of "the balance of
power," on which modern European politics are
founded. He warned us not to enter into any entangling alliances, to avoid and keep out of all
schemes of conquest and territorial aggrandizement, — at least until both the country and its institutions were thoroughly consolidated and matured.
His great idea was to see his country free from political connection with every other country, independent of all, and under the influence of none. He
was, in the fullest sense of the word, a great and
true American. He liked Americanism, without
any hyphens.

Wisely have our people and statesmen heeded

his words. Even in 1898, that wonderful year full of events which have turned the world inside out and shifted history from the Atlantic to the Pacific, the American people did not and will not depart from the true idea of Washington, even though they extend their domain and set up democratic institutions in the Pacific.

The American is by true inheritance a soldier, but a soldier of righteousness. The Puritans, first in Holland and then in Britain, believed in necessary war as an instrument of divine justice. Colonists from many countries in Europe and representatives of various races came to these shores and have been fused into one grand American composite. Yet those who laid the foundations, planned the structure, and formed the ideas under which our nation has grown, were men who asserted the principle of personal freedom. They read the open Bible and interpreted it for themselves. They believed in the right to punish or depose their rulers when these were not faithful. Like Cromwell and the British people, they believed in strong nations helping the weak and oppressed peoples. They held to the Hebrew and Puritan principle that war might be employed as the instrument of God for justice and righteousness. Washington's maxim was "In time of peace prepare for war."

Furthermore, they believed in asserting true manliness. They would not allow the bully to rage, or the tyrant in church or state to have his own way. Without virility and personal courage, they considered all other gifts and graces vain. So from Massachusetts to Georgia, Puritan, Hollander, Cavalier, Huguenot, and all believers in good government, living as they did betwixt the ocean and the Indian, between the land forces and the fleets of hostile Europeans, were bred to the use of arms. They had before them the example of the great motherland, of whom Shakespeare says: —

> "This England never did and never shall
> Lie at the proud foot of a conqueror
> But when it first did help to wound itself."

But, when Thomas Dekker wrote the lines in "Old Fortunatus,"

> "And though mine arm should conquer twenty worlds,
> There's a lean fellow beats all conquerors,"

did he have in his mind's eye the long and lank figure, whom Europe has so often caricatured as tall, strong, and wiry, without rotundity, but not lacking avoirdupois, "Uncle Sam"?

CHAPTER II.

FROM LEXINGTON TO STILLWATER.

THE American colonial soldier was a young man from the farmhouse or the town dwelling. In politics, before the Declaration of Independence, he was a loyal Englishman, standing on his rights as English law had defined them. If at Lexington the Minuteman had to fight the king's troops, who first fired on him, he went the next day and took affidavit that he was a law-abiding citizen, defending himself against the lawless military that had interfered with his rights on the king's highway. The Continental soldier resisted revolution from without. He took this name, because he was more and more interested in what all the colonies did in union, and less in what the king's ministers were pleased to dictate. Devout though he was, he had a new idea, or rather an old one, which was always latent in the Hebrew commonwealth and the Christian church before Latin domination and absolutism grew up. It was the idea of a state without a king and a church free from politics. He even believed in good coinage without the use of the divine name.

In his state militia regiment, the soldier of '76 was usually a hero in homespun, without much idea of uniform. Only slowly did he come into rigid discipline, and that for the sake of the cause. The musket used by him in the national warfare was more apt to be his own gun, which had hung on pegs over the fireplace, with which he had shot birds, squirrels, deer, and bears. His home, by the Delaware or the Merrimac, was a plain building of logs or timber, with a well-sweep and woodpile outside, and indoors an open fireplace furnished with iron pothooks and andirons, with a living room in which were wooden settle and chairs. Over the mantelpiece stood candlesticks and a few books, which were pretty apt to be of solid character. Above, on the wall, or set on deer horns, was his firelock, which, with his trusty axe, was his familiar tool.

When the Continental army of regulars was formed, the men wore buff and blue, cloth of the latter and trimmings of the former, with top-boots, knickerbockers, and woollen stockings. Metal buttons, though comparatively new things, were plenty on cuffs, shirt, and front. Over his coat and waistcoat were two broad straps crossed diagonally. These held up his cartridge box and bayonet scabbard. On his head was a three-cornered or cocked hat with cockade or pompon of red, white, and blue.

His powder-horn, for loading and priming, was carved with sentiments, dates, scraps, history, statistics, or geography — his true "horn-book." His musket was a smooth bore, with a wood or iron ramrod. The cock held a piece of flint, which struck upon a steel fender and threw sparks at the priming powder in the pan below. Hearty and healthy, alert, potent, brave was the young Minuteman and Continental. Most of the civil leaders and military officers of the Revolution were young men.

Until regular army firearms and bayonets were imported from Europe, mostly from the Netherlands and France, the ordinary soldier in the ranks knew very little about a bayonet. The rifle was first in use among the Pennsylvanians, Swiss and Germans. It was superbly developed in Kentucky. Morgan's riflemen and sharpshooters were recruited almost wholly in the region where the Swiss and Germans from the Palatinate had settled. Our gallant Marine Corps was the first part of the armed force, or permanent military establishment created by law. It is thus the oldest part of the war service of the United States.

The conflict of arms between the years 1775 and 1783 was a civil war between kinsmen who spoke the same language. It was hard work for the British king to get natives for his work, and he had to hire foreigners. If in the American army were many who did not talk English well, there were in the royal forces Hessians and Indians who could not speak it at all. About forty thousand loyalists, or people who served King George, left our borders for Canada, and living there, developed that region.

After the Declaration of Independence, the scene of war was transferred from the neighborhood of Boston to the region of Manhattan Island. A great British fleet and army under Lord Howe entered the Hudson River, to separate New England from the other colonies and then meet Burgoyne coming from Canada. Thirty thousand splendidly armed and equipped British and German soldiers tried to surround and capture eighteen thousand Americans, most of them raw militia without guns or supplies.

The British plan of campaign was to march an army down the Hudson valley from Canada and unite forces on Manhattan Island, cutting the thirteen colonies in half, and thus quickly ending the war. Washington's strategy was to keep the two armies separate, by drawing Lord Howe's forces southward; and Washington succeeded even in disaster. The two British hosts were never united, and the colonies were never separated. This is the whole story of the war.

In the battle of Brooklyn, August 27, 1776, the brave young men of the Maryland line bore the brunt of the British attack. They were overwhelmed by superior force. Washington relieved Putnam and his nine thousand men, and in a fog escaped with his army across the Hudson. Losing an important fort through a deserter's treachery and the assault of the Hessians, Washington retreated to New Jersey with his remnant of brave men. He crossed the Delaware on the 8th of December at Trenton and reached Pennsylvania again, the state where his earliest, longest, and most glorious service had been, or was to be.

When Christmas Day dawned, it was still dark night with the cause of freedom. Neither New Englanders nor New York Dutch folks then celebrated the birthday of Jesus. The former had their Thanksgiving festival in November, and the latter, Santa Claus Day, December 6. But the Germans, whether Hessians forced to fight for King George, or the older makers of Pennsylvania, from whom we have borrowed the Christmas tree, until it is now national, always made much of Christmas. Among the soldiers there was much hilarity and carousing. Washington knew this and resolved to cross the Delaware again and attack Colonel Rahl's Germans. His Massachusetts men from Marblehead pushed the boats through the floating ice. The Pennsylvania colonel, Jehu Eyre, Washington's aid, directed the general movement, and the successful crossing of the ice-choked river was more wonderful than the battle itself. With scarcely the loss of a man, Washington captured a thousand Hessian prisoners, plenty of arms and ammunition, infusing a novel sort of Christmas joy all through the new nation. The prisoners, sent among their Pennsylvania German kinsmen, who could talk their language, had their eyes opened, and many of them deserted. After the war many more remained in or came back to America, where among their descendants are to-day thousands of fine families. Our brilliant cavalry leader, General Custer, was the grandson of a Hessian.

Then grandly Philadelphia's young men, led by the "free Quakers," Colonels Jehu and Manuel Eyre, rushed to the aid of Washington. Lord Cornwallis, a gay fox-hunter, having hastened across New Jersey to catch Washington and his raw reënforcements, waited over night at Trenton with only the Assinpink creek between the two camps. He expected to "bag" his game in the morning. He had left part of his force at Princeton, where, as we shall see, one of the decisive battles of the Revolution was to be fought. But in the night, leaving his watch-fires burning, Washington moved around to the eastward, over an old and shorter road, but now frozen hard. As the morning sun arose, his advanced guard was on the crest of the hill near

Princeton. The regiment or two of redcoats on their way to Trenton met the Americans. The brave British lads marched up, fired their volley; then, with a cheer, they rushed upon the Americans and drove them flying.

At this moment Washington appeared in fiery valor. With the soldier's splendid enthusiasm, and knowing that if beaten the American cause was lost, he led his men, veterans and Philadelphia militia, to the charge. He plunged into the smoke and rode up to within thirty yards of the British firing line. For a few minutes, invisible and liable to be shot from either side, his officers were anxious enough. Then the wind blew away the cloud. There he stood unscathed, making a living picture, which Trumbull the painter transferred from reality to canvas. Mainly through the bravery of the Philadelphia troops and artillerymen, the battle became a great victory. In this conflict Colonel Jehu Eyre was Washington's aid.

Drawing off his troops to Morristown, New Jersey, Washington spent the winter there. He had won his point in keeping the British scattered. In the spring, officers from France, Holland, Germany, and Poland came over to help us, among whom were the French Marquis de Lafayette; the Dutch naval officers, Commodore Dillon and Captain Joyner, and the army men, Colonel Dircks and

Bernard Romans; the Germans Baron de Kalb and
Baron Steuben, the Polish Count Pulaski, and others.
To meet Lord Howe's fleet and army at New
York, General Burgoyne had come down from
Canada through the valley and waterway of Lake
Champlain, Lake George Valley, and the Hudson
River; but through the activity of General Philip
Schuyler, who cut off his supplies, his forces were
nearly reduced to starvation. The failure of the
expedition to Oswego, the defeat of the Hessians
at Bennington by the militia of New Hampshire
and Vermont, the American success in the fiercely
contested battle of Oriskany in the Mohawk Valley,
— one of the bloodiest conflicts during the war, —
compelled Burgoyne, after fighting battles at Bemis
Heights and Stillwater, to surrender his entire army
of six thousand men. The total loss of the British
was about ten thousand, and their plan of campaign
was completely ruined.

Thus New England and New York were left un-
vexed by British steel or keel. Within two centuries, into the domain bounded by that Empire State
which was born in 1777, four powers had come and
three had gone. In 1880, when the people of the
First Reformed Church of Schenectady celebrated
their bicentennial anniversary, a colossal banner,
quartered in green, orange, red, and white, represent-
ing the turtle, the totem of the Iroquois; the pelican

feeding her young with bosom-blood, the emblem used by William the Silent; the British lion; and the American eagle, told the romance of conquest in graphic symbol.

In the South, after fighting the battle of Brandywine and another at Germantown, in both of which the Americans were beaten, the British army settled down quietly in Philadelphia. Washington went into winter quarters at Valley Forge.

CHAPTER III.

THE NAVY IN THE REVOLUTIONARY WAR.

IT is generally supposed that in the Revolutionary war our liberties were won entirely by the army on land. Yet it is even more probable that, from 1775 to 1783, there were more Americans fighting for their country on the seas than there were on shore. It was not the victories of the Continental troops which made King George sue for peace, so much as it was the captures of British ships and the injury to British commerce wrought by our men-of-war and privateers.

Although the war of independence opened with spirit and was carried on with courage and self-devotion, yet there were great fluctuations in patriotism and in the size of the army, as well as in the sums of money spent for defence. The high-water mark of the national spirit was reached in those efforts which compelled the surrender of Burgoyne. Then, both Americans and Europeans thought the war would end, but it did not. Disasters to our arms followed, which made the public spirit droop, until it looked as though we should have to depend upon Frenchmen to win our liberties for us. The American army was very large at the beginning. In 1776 there was probably as many as ninety thousand militia and regulars, on paper at least, and nearly fifty thousand were actually under arms, but in 1781 the number had fallen to about fourteen thousand, and the money paid annually for military support had decreased from $21,000,000 to $2,000,000.

With dissensions in Congress and in the state legislatures, the people discouraged and tired of the war, it is probable that had it not been for our navy's influence upon British opinion, we could not, even with Bourbon aid, have won our independence. But with our privateers and men-of-war at sea capturing hundreds of British vessels, marine insurance in London rose to forty and even sixty per cent. In one year only forty out of four hundred British vessels engaged in the African trade escaped the clutches of the Americans. In another year, half the trading fleet between Great Britain and the West Indies was taken. As matter of fact, it was the clamor of the British merchants and their pressure upon the government which compelled King George to make peace.

Beside the Continental or national navy, most of the states had their own ships and fleets, Massachusetts, Pennsylvania, and South Carolina leading. The Bay State commissioned during the war about six hundred privateers, and her own vessels probably outnumbered those of the national navy. South Carolina had the heaviest ship afloat that ever, before 1812, sailed under the American flag, though unfortunately she was captured by the British. The Pennsylvanian, *Hyder Ally*, fought one of the most brilliant battles of the war.

Our men went to sea as soon as hostilities opened at Lexington, and began destroying British commerce in the African and West Indian waters. The Tories were also very busy. In one year they had as many as six thousand men serving the king in privateers, which in six months brought into port 142 prizes. The most active naval year was 1777, when as many possibly as eight hundred captures were made on one side or the other. It is believed that during the whole war there were about five thousand naval war episodes, including captures, armed encounters on the coast or in the rivers, or bloody battles at sea, in which about three thousand prizes were captured from the enemy.

At the beginning of the war, under John Adams, the great nationalizer, thirteen frigates, named after the different states, were ordered to be built. The chief object at first was defence, and to intercept supplies for the British army, but after the Declaration of Independence, the purpose was offensive as well as defensive. Then, not only were the Continental armies and militia to be supplied with clothing and munitions of war, but the enemy was to be weakened as much as possible. Both objects were grandly accomplished, for most of the cannon, mortars, and powder used in our army was made for us in Great Britain and captured by our sailors.

After the British had left Boston, Captain Mudford in the *Franklin* captured a ship that had on board fifteen hundred barrels of powder, intrenching tools, gun carriages, and other stores. In one prize Captain Jones found ten thousand British suits of clothing. In another, Commodore Hopkins captured eight out of ten ships which were being sent with men and stores to Georgia. An entire fleet was fitted out in Boston harbor by stores meant for the British army in New York, but captured on their way. The great headquarters of our privateers from 1775 until 1781 was at the Dutch island of St. Eustatius in the West Indies.

"Maine" has become a synonym with the beginning of hostilities in three of our wars, British, Barbary, and Spanish. The first Lexington on the seas was, like the opening battle on land, "a rising of the people against a regular force, and was characterized by a long chase, a bloody struggle, and a triumph." In this the armed schooner *Margaretta* was captured, May 11, 1775, near Machias, in Maine, by an enterprising party of forty young men. Washington issued commissions to vessels to cruise in Massachusetts Bay, and intercept the British supply-ships. Captain Manly in the schooner *Lee* at Marblehead took the English brig *Nancy* and three other store-ships, which helped finely to supply the Continentals with munitions of war.

Although for the United States to begin naval war with so powerful a country as Great Britain was like "an infant taking a bull by the horns," yet with Hercules's precedent of success, Congress began equipping a navy, and made Esek Hopkins of Rhode Island commander-in-chief. Gradually our little cruisers got out to sea and captured not only prizes, but even British vessels of war. Yet it was very difficult to create a navy, in the real sense of the term, and as we now understand it. Owing to the suddenness of the war and the total check to commerce, thousands of sailors had enlisted in the army or entered as privateersmen. This took away so many of our seafaring people that the national navy could not be easily manned. Nevertheless, Captain Paul Jones secured and drilled a crew, and in the United States sloop of war *Providence* took sixteen prizes. Captain Whipple, with one ship, captured ten merchant vessels in a fleet of fifty. Captain Biddle in the *Andrea Dorea* took so many of the enemy's armed vessels and merchantmen, putting prize crews on each, that when he came back from his cruise, only five of his original crew were with him, the places of his own sailors being supplied by volunteers from among the prisoners.

To show how British plans were often upset by our sea-rovers, we may state that within a few weeks of 1776, about five hundred men of one of the best corps in the British army were, with all their equipments and stores, captured by our little ships of war. These were for the most part light vessels armed with from five to twenty guns, four, six, or twelve pounders. The benefit of these captures was twofold. They not only weakened the enemy, but they gave Congress so many prisoners, that the British could not look upon our men as rebels only and refuse to exchange on equal terms, but were obliged to treat them as equals.

The *Reprisal* was the first American man-of-war to get to Europe, arriving in France in 1776 with Dr. Benjamin Franklin as passenger. The doings of the *Providence, Lexington, Andrea Dorea, Defense, Lee,* and other vessels caused intense surprise and indignation in England; for people travelling from London to Holland or France ran the risk of capture by American privateers. With the great thoroughfares of the sea thus threatened, marine insurance rose to an enormous amount. All England was so alarmed that some of the great county fairs were not held, and freights were sent to the continent in French ships.

The *Andrea Dorea*, Captain Robinson, after carrying a copy of the Declaration of Independence to St. Eustatius, received, on November 16, 1776, the first salute ever fired in honor of the American flag by a foreign power. Five days afterward, Captain Isaac Van Bibber, in *The Baltimore Hero*, captured an English brigantine just outside the harbor. On her way home the *Andrea Dorea* captured the *Race Horse*, an English man-of-war, that had been sent out to capture her. Captain Robinson brought his prize into the Delaware River, but when the British fleet came in, this gallant vessel had to be burnt to save her from the enemy.

In fact, all along our coast and in the Hudson and Delaware rivers, there were battles or skirmishes, whenever a British cruiser appeared or attempted to land. On lakes George and Champlain, flotillas of boats were built and armed, and a battle fought October 11, 1776. The American vessels, *Royal Savage, Revenge, Liberty, Lee, Congress, Washington, Trumbull*, with eight gondolas, in all manned by six hundred men and carrying ninety guns, which fired at one discharge six hundred and forty-seven pounds, met with the British force of thirty fighting vessels. A hot fire of several hours was the result, in which about a hundred were killed and wounded on both sides. This battle on Lake Champlain was renewed the next day by General Arnold, who fought with great bravery. Though the Americans lost eleven vessels, and the affair was disastrous, much credit was gained our arms by the obstinacy and bravery of our men.

In 1777 we had something like a regular navy, though at the assault on Fort Mifflin in the Delaware, by the British squadron, our men were obliged to evacuate the work. The enemy got possession of the river, from Cape May to Philadelphia, and several of our ships were burned to prevent them from falling into his hands. The British vessels were blockading our ports and it was difficult to get the national ships at sea. This was the year when the stars were first added to the stripes in our national flag. It is claimed that the first American vessel to fly the striped flag of the Continental Congress in foreign waters, and to salute it with cannon, was the brig *Nancy*, late in July, 1776, whose captain, while at St. Thomas in the West Indies, heard of the Declaration of Independence, signed a few days before. The first to float the starry flag on a regular American man-of-war in alien seas was Commodore Paul Jones of endless fame.

CHAPTER IV.

FROM SARATOGA TO YORKTOWN.

BENJAMIN FRANKLIN went to France as envoy of the Continental Congress, and there made many friends. When asked in Paris about the success of the American republic, he always answered smilingly, *Ça ira* (it will go). These words, afterward taken as the name of French warships and privateers, became a cheery cry of encouragement when things looked dark. The phrase is still used by the French people.

And it did go. The Bourbon king and government, in the hope of regaining Canada, and in order to humble Albion their foe, recognized our country, saluted our flag, which then had thirteen stripes but no stars, lent us three million dollars, gave us two million dollars more, and agreed to help us with an army and a fleet. The German Baron Steuben, a superb drill-master, reached Valley Forge, and by his diligence and pains changed a mob of militia into a splendid army. Soon, at Monmouth, for the first time in the war, a regular pitched battle between two well-organized armies was to be fought.

No war can be carried on without money. Robert Morris, the Philadelphia banker, provided "the sinews of war" by personally collecting money and pledging his own credit. He was the great financier of the Revolution. Another friend of Washington and our country was the Philadelphia German "Baker General" Christopher Ludwick, who set up ovens, made good bread in the camps, and otherwise improved the food of our soldiers.

When the French fleet sailed to America, the British were forced to leave Philadelphia, and fifteen thousand of them started to go by land across the Jerseys. On the way to Monmouth hundreds of Hessians deserted. A fierce battle was fought, and then Washington retired to the line of the Hudson River.

Meanwhile the Iroquois Indians had taken the side of the British, and in central New York and Pennsylvania devastated the country. They made raids in the Mohawk, Schoharie, and Wallkill valleys, and massacred the people at Wyoming and Cherry Valley. On the other hand, in Illinois and Indiana, Captain George Rogers Clark drove the British and their red allies before him, held the territory, and thus gave solid ground for the Continental Congress to claim this region at the peace of 1783. Toward the end of the year 1778 the British captured Savannah. In midsummer of 1779 General

Anthony Wayne performed the most brilliant feat of the whole war. By a bayonet charge, he took Stony Point on the Hudson. After this, with the exception of the episode of Arnold's treason at West Point, the awful winter suffering at Morristown, and Arnold's raid in Connecticut, there were no military events of importance in the North, except Sullivan's expedition into the lake country of New York.

Arnold and Montgomery's expedition in Canada and the invasion of an Indian wilderness in 1779 were like making war in a foreign country. The latter was beyond the line of coast settlements, and the roads following the Indian trails had to be chopped through the woods and made wide enough for the artillery. The expedition was a necessity, in order to prevent further Indian incursions and to stop a destructive "fire in the rear." It was decided to destroy the Indian settlements.

Washington ordered General Sullivan to march from Easton on the Delaware to Wyoming on the Susquehanna, and thence northward, while a brigade of General James Clinton moved from Otsego Lake southward to join Sullivan.

No other state in the Union has such a series of waterways, salt and fresh, inland and oceanic, as New York, which was the real centre of the war, and contributed 43,600 soldiers, in this respect being surpassed only by Massachusetts. Right in the heart of the commonwealth is a wonderful lake region. Beginning with Onondaga, we have a dozen of these sheets of fresh water, most of them so long and narrow that they are called "finger lakes." All lovely and beautiful, they lie directly over beds of salt or above intervening strata, under which is the deposit of an ocean that dried up ages ago. How these lakes were made, whether by the scooping and scouring action of glaciers, or by the melting out of the salt caverns, and the breaking of the rocky shell above them, thus letting in the water and making deep the troughs on the earth's surface, is not known. Among these lakes the Six Nations of the Iroquois lived.

The march of Sullivan's united forces began August 26, 1779. On the 29th the big battle of Newtown, near Elmira, was fought and won. Then the Indian villages on Cayuga and Seneca lakes, with their grain fields, orchards, and long houses, were destroyed. After going as far as Canandaigua, the army of thirty-five hundred men returned, having so devastated the Indian region that the Iroquois could never again during the war give serious trouble. They retreated to Canada, and there disease and famine reduced their numbers terribly. Six American counties are named after Sullivan, the brave soldier of Irish descent. On our side of the boundary line the name of Brandt, the Indian chief, whose warriors raided the valleys of New York and Pennsylvania, is a synonym of cruelty and terror. On the other stands his statue, and he is honored. The war between the New York frontiersmen and the Tories, Indian and British, was prolonged, bitter, and bloody. Only one other state, Massachusetts, excelled New York in the number of enlistments or soldiers in the field.

In the South, although the British forces had taken Charleston on the 12th of May, 1780, the "swamp fox," Marion, gave them much trouble. The redcoats marched inland to Camden. There, on the 16th of August, they won a victory; but in October the triumph of the Kentuckians at King's Mountain changed the whole face of affairs. The American highlanders, living on the borders of North and South Carolina and in Kentucky and Tennessee, had formed a body of rough riders, and quickly marching eastward attacked their foes. Although the latter were partially equipped with breech-loading arms, among the first employed in warfare, and had bayonets, the rough riders, who had neither, though they knew their rifles well, won a splendid victory.

General Greene of Rhode Island began to be master of the situation, for he led Cornwallis on a lively chase after him into Virginia. Morgan and his riflemen gained the battle of Cowpens. Then, although at Guilford Court House, Cornwallis drove back the Americans, he had to retreat and so began marching toward Petersburg, Virginia. Greene, with an army of only two thousand men, but helped by Marion, Sumter, and Pickens, won victories at Camden and Eutaw Springs.

During all the time of the Revolution the Dutch were our friends. They recognized us and lent us more money even than the French did, helping us also with ships and men. At the island of St. Eustatius, in the West Indies, on November 16, 1776, they were the first Europeans to salute our flag of thirteen stripes. They supplied liberally our privateers and men-of-war, so that probably one-half of the regular equipments and ammunition which came from Europe to the Continental army were imported through the Dutch at St. Eustatius. Indeed, the British government thought it so necessary to destroy this place of aid and comfort to Americans that Rodney's big fleet was sent to the West Indies, instead of having him go to the help of Cornwallis, who badly needed assistance.

General Greene having recovered the Carolinas, and La Fayette having pressed him hard, Cornwallis was forced to retreat to Yorktown, where he fortified himself. The French fleet under Count de Grasse had arrived, and "the sparkling Bourbonnieres," as the French soldiers in white and red were called, were encamped at Lebanon, Connecticut, where Washington often took counsel with "Brother Jonathan," as Governor Trumbull was called. The French wanted to attack Canada, hoping thus to regain it for themselves; but Washington preferred, even after war was over, to have English instead of French neighbors. So he planned, with the aid of our French allies, to march south to Yorktown and capture Cornwallis.

Having French and Dutch financial aid and promises, Robert Morris was able to collect money for the expedition. The men in buff and blue and their allies in white and red moved together to the head of the Chesapeake Bay. Here they took ships to Yorktown. Rodney, having left Cornwallis in his trap, captured St. Eustatius, with all its Dutch and American stores, its two thousand American sailors, and twenty-six American privateers and war vessels. He wasted his time on the beach, auctioneering off the spoils, instead of coming to help Cornwallis, who, after three weeks of siege, surrendered.

Although this was practically the end of the war, nearly two years of inaction and waiting were necessary before the peace treaty was signed. While our Continental army lay at Newburg, such was the dissatisfaction with Congress that a plot was formed to establish a monarchy, but the Dutch loans of money deposited at Cornwall came in good season to pay off officers and troops, and keep them contented until the peace treaty was signed. On April 19th the army was disbanded, the war of the Revolution lasting exactly eight years.

Thus ended the existence of the Continental soldier, who stood for something much more valuable than either the money or the Congress of the same name. In the course of the war the quality of the men composing the Congress gradually deteriorated, while the paper money grew so worthless that a bagful of it was necessary to pay for a dinner or the grooming of a horse. The old slang phrase, " Don't care a continental," referred to a bit of pasteboard called money, and not to the brave soldier in buff and blue.

CHAPTER V.

THE STARS AND STRIPES IN THE MEDITERRANEAN.

WHEN, in 1778, the French became our allies, the marine policy of the United States was greatly changed. Instead of trying to build ships at home, under great difficulties, heavier expense, and with larger chances of capture by the British before they were launched, it was now possible to build or buy war vessels abroad. The splendid ship *Alliance*, constructed at Salisbury, in Massachusetts, was named to commemorate our friendship with France, and became the favorite of the nation. Since her day there has always been a ship in our navy named like herself. Other vessels were the *Confederacy*, the *Hague*, *Queen of France*, *Ranger*, *Gates*, and *Saratoga*. Captain Paul Jones, in command of the *Providence*, twelve guns, harried the Irish coast and then crossed over to the English waters to alarm the enemy at home. The next year, 1779, he was given a larger command, and a project was made for making a descent upon Liverpool with a body of troops commanded by La Fayette, but as nothing came of this, Paul Jones went on board the *Bon*

Homme Richard, which was named in compliment to Dr. Franklin.

This ship was, in its way, an old curiosity shop. It was as strangely manned as it was built, for the variety of its people suggested a rag bag or a crazy-quilt. The ship was quite old, built many years before as an Indiaman, and had one of those high, old-fashioned poops that made the stern look like a tower. The whole vessel resembled an enormous Japanese junk. Six old 18-pound cannon were mounted below and a battery of 12-pounders was put on the main gun-deck, while on the quarter-deck and forecastle were eight 9-pounders, making a mixed and rather light armament of forty-two guns.

Except the few American officers, the crew was made up of English, Irish, Scotch, Welsh, Germans, Swedes, Norwegians, Portuguese, Spaniards, and even Malays. The 135 marines on board were expected to keep the sailors in order, but were about as much mixed as to nationality as were the seamen. Indeed, the *Bon Homme Richard* of 1779, with its complement of 380 souls, presented in miniature a picture of the various kinds of people that are being made into American citizens to-day. Nevertheless, with this ship and company, Paul Jones kept the eastern coast of England in terror during many months. Families along shore buried their silver plate, and both the military and marines were kept in a state of constant drill and expectation. Jones took about twenty-five prizes, one of which, curiously enough, was a brigantine named the *Mayflower*, which he captured near the place whence the Pilgrims, in 1609, fled in their boats from bishop-ridden England over to Holland.

More wonderful to relate, Jones with his rickety old ship captured one of the finest vessels in the British navy. The *Serapis* was a double-decked, fifty-gun ship, new and strong and fast. She mounted on her lower gun-deck twenty 18-pounders, on her upper gun-deck twenty 9-pounders, and on her quarter-deck and forecastle ten 6-pounders. Her regularly trained crew consisted of 320 men, fifteen of whom were Lascars, or natives of India. The *Serapis* had yellow, the *Richard* had black sides.

The two men-of-war, the *Serapis* and *Countess of Scarborough*, were convoying the Baltic fleet of forty-one ships. Of the vessels in Jones's squadron, the *Richard* fought the *Serapis* alone.

The battle began about dark, but by and by the moon rose, and toward eight o'clock the two ships were near enough to open fire. Although the Americans were fighting against a greatly superior force, yet Paul Jones had infused his own spirit into his men, and they went cheerfully to their quarters.

At the very first broadside two of his old 18-pounders burst, blowing up the deck above and killing or wounding nearly all the men below. This caused the heavy battery to be deserted, so that now there was to be a fight between a 12-pounder and an 18-pounder frigate. According to the naval axiom of those days the 12-pounder frigate could never hope to win. So certain was the English commander of his speedy victory that, when the two vessels got foul of each other, Captain Pearson called out, —

"Have you struck your colors?"

The answer immediately came back, "I have not yet begun to fight."

The ships were lashed together and the combat continued to rage. Down below the 18-pounder guns of the *Serapis* soon blew in and blew out large pieces of the old ship *Richard's* sides, until the British balls beat only the air, but on the upper gun-deck the Americans were pouring in shot and grape, while aloft in the tops their musket-men swept the decks and cleared the crow's nests of the *Serapis* with their fire, until all the British got below deck. Boldly climbing out on the main-yards of the *Richard*, the Americans dropped hand grenades down through the hatchways of the *Serapis*, by which they exploded the loose ammunition which the powder boys had carelessly left uncovered.

By this calamity twenty men were killed and thirty-eight wounded, or in other words nearly sixty persons disabled.

In this curious night battle the English were all fighting with the heavy cannon below, while the Americans were working the upper-deck guns and small arms. The *Richard* was on fire several times, but the flames were put out. When, however, it was reported that she was sinking, the one hundred or more British prisoners on board the *Richard* were released to save their lives. One of these got on board the *Serapis* and informed Captain Pearson that the *Richard* was sinking. The English leader, expecting to take his enemy, called the boarders with the idea of ordering them on the *Richard's* deck, but seeing the Americans all ready to repel the attack the pikemen retreated. Meanwhile the English prisoners on the *Richard* were set to work at the pumps.

Both ships again caught fire, and warriors had to turn firemen. After this the American cannonade began to increase and that of the *Serapis* to slacken. About one hour after the explosion the British flag was struck. As not one of his men would expose himself to the fire from the *Richard's* tops, Captain Pearson hauled down the colors himself.

This terrible battle lasted nearly four hours. The *Richard* was so nearly knocked to pieces that her upper decks and poop were almost ready to fall into the gunroom below, all except a few supports being shot away. On fire most of the time, she was now sinking. Yet by removing the powder from the deck, and keeping men at the pumps all night, the flames were got under at about ten o'clock next morning. During the day the wounded were removed to the *Serapis*, and about nine o'clock of the 25th the *Bon Homme Richard* went down bow foremost. In this awful slaughter probably one-half of all that were engaged were killed or wounded. Paul Jones rigged up jury masts on the *Serapis*, and with his two prizes got into the Texel, in North Holland, on the 6th of October.

The Hollanders were delighted with this victory, and the praises of Paul Jones were sung from one end of the Dutch United States to the other. The sentiment of the republic against Great Britain ripened, and sympathy with Americans deepened, until at last the Netherlanders became our allies and friends and declared war against Great Britain, lending us money and otherwise giving us aid. When I was in Amsterdam in September, 1898, after seeing Queen Wilhelmina inaugurated in the Nieuwe Kerk, I heard the people in the street singing their old historic songs, and among them "Hier komt Paul Jones aan" (Here comes along Paul Jones).

The year 1779 was marked by much naval activity. There were numerous naval battles and captures of prizes. A great expedition of twenty vessels, with fifteen hundred soldiers, was despatched from Massachusetts to dislodge the British who had a strong post upon the Penobscot River. These light ships, however, were not able to contend with the heavy British frigates, and the expedition came to disaster and caused naval enterprises to cease for some time. Furthermore, the British were so embittered against our privateers that they took two methods of annihilating, if possible, the American marine. They refused to exchange any more of the seamen which they had captured. They thus accumulated in England a large body of prisoners, who were kept at Dartmoor and other well-guarded places until the war was over. On the other hand, they authorized the employment of no fewer than eighty-five thousand men in their navy, to make sure of annihilating ours.

Nevertheless, on June 2, 1780, there was a terrible battle of two hours and a half, a real "yard-arm engagement," between the *Trumbull* and the *Watt*, the former having thirty guns and the latter thirty-four. In the way of a regular cannonade this was thought to be the severest battle in the naval war of the Revolution. Soon after this, the *Saratoga* fought the *Charming Mollie* and captured her.

This victory was gained by the pike, Lieutenant Joshua Barney leading the boarders, and overcoming on the *Charming Mollie's* deck a British party nearly double his own. Later on the *Trumbull* was captured by the British vessels, the *Iris* and the *General Monk*.

The *Hyder Ally* was a Pennsylvania state ship, under command of Lieutenant Joshua Barney, and named after a Hindoo chieftain who in India had opposed his conquerors.

It had been fitted out to keep the Delaware River free from British barges and small cruisers, and to convoy ships in and out the waters around Cape May. Barney captured the British privateer, named the *Fair American*, and putting on board a prize crew sent her up the river. He next fought and took the *General Monk*, a twenty-gun ship. This action was thought to be one of the most brilliant that ever occurred under the American flag, for the *Monk* was heavier and larger and carried 9-pounder guns, while the *Hyder Ally* had only 6-pounders.

The regular naval warfare came to an end under Captain Manly, who on our side may be said almost to have begun it, for this gallant officer commanded, as we saw, the schooner *Lee*, which on November 29, 1775, captured the British brig *Nancy* and other store-ships.

It is a brilliant story, that of our little navy during the Revolutionary War. But as "life without letters is death," so unless a story is well told it is not known. It is no wonder that the average American has a very hazy idea, if any at all, about the great work done and the decisive influence upon results, which our fathers on the sea wrought during Revolutionary days.

We must never forget the heroes — Hopkins, Wickes, Conyngham, Biddle, Nicholson, Manly, Barney, Whipple, O'Brien, Robinson, Paul Jones, Barry, and others, beside the French and Dutch captains — who helped us. Nor should we fail to remember the gallant men of the shore and the seaports, and the marines, who, though not known, did their part to serve their country. One who looks over the register of names in our navy to-day, and along through its history, will find that certain families, like the Nicholsons, Rodgers, and Perrys, have contributed a large number of competent and gallant officers, who in the naval service have shed lustre upon their country. With not a few their line of service is ancestral, beginning even back in the Revolution.

There were many prophetic voices concerning the United States of America. Van der Capellen, one of our many steadfast friends, declared that the Teutonic race in crossing the Atlantic gained potency of five hundred years of progress. The Spanish minister in London, in 1783, used words that are worth recalling. He said: —

"The federal republic is born a pygmy. A day will come when it will be a giant, even a colossus, formidable in these countries. Liberty of conscience, the facility of establishing a new population on immense lands, as well as the advantages of a new government, will draw thither farmers and artisans from all nations. In a few years we will watch with grief the tyrannical existence of this same colossus."

How truly fulfilled in 1898!

The little baby boy Simon Bolivar, destined to be the liberator of Spanish America, was forty days old when the treaty between the two English-speaking nations was signed.

CHAPTER VI.

FROM CONFEDERATION TO CONSTITUTION.

AFTER the Revolutionary War several years of misery and distress followed. The nation created by the Declaration of Independence of July 4, 1776, was a headless republic, a mere league of states. They could hold together as long as there was war, but broke into quarrelling sections as soon as the pressure of foreign hostility was removed. Europeans, even Englishmen, laughed at the idea of "federal government" ever being successful on a large scale. For a little scrap of land, among the mountains of Switzerland, it might work. Possibly even in the swampy Netherlands it might do, but in a great country, with plenty of land, never. Large republics hitherto had been only ideals in imagination. So they watched to see the American confederation fall to pieces.

Congress had no power and there was no centre of authority. With plenty of paper, but little gold or silver, nearly every one was in debt. There was no free interstate commerce, and affairs were drifting into a dreadful condition. In western Massachusetts, which had a war debt of $4,000,000, things came to a head in what is called Shays's Rebellion. Many hundred excited farmers tried to stop all lawsuits for debt. They claimed that the taxes were too heavy, the lawyers too extortionate, and the governors and senators too aristocratic; that the capital ought to be removed from Boston; and that plenty of paper money should be issued. The militia quelled the uprising, reforms were begun, and Shays fled. Being a revolutionary soldier, he lived in New York state under a government pension. His Massachusetts mob gave a tremendous impulse to the movement for a better general government.

The strong motive that held the states together was the claims of ownership in land, which several of them held and which they hoped to sell. They would thus get money for the payment of their heavy war debts. The states owed $26,000,000 and the United States $42,000,000. Massachusetts, Connecticut, New York, and the Southern States, except Maryland, claimed the country west of them as far as the Mississippi River. Probably the reason why the other six states did not make a similar claim was that their western boundaries were already fixed. These were Rhode Island, New Hampshire, and the well-surveyed states of Pennsylvania and those touching it, New Jersey, Delaware, and Maryland. The best-founded claim was that of New

York, which had gained its right to the soil by well-attested treaties with its first owners, the Iroquois nation. No other state has so large a collection of Indian deeds and wampum documents, given by red men for lands sold, which take the place of written and sealed parchments and papers among white men.

New York led the way to the settlement of the question. She was soon joined by Massachusetts, Connecticut, and Virginia. They agreed to give the land northwest of the Ohio River and between the lakes and the Mississippi, in area larger than the Austrian Empire, to the United States, for the general welfare. Congress created a body of laws, very liberal in character, ruling out slavery, and all bigotry and political churchism. Thereupon began an emigration of people from the Eastern and Middle States into this splendid territory, out of which Ohio, Indiana, Illinois, Michigan, and Wisconsin have been formed.

The pressing national want was "a more perfect union." In order to form this delegates were summoned from the different states, and a body of very able men convened in Philadelphia. After four months of debate in secret session, they agreed upon a written constitution. Thomas Jefferson was absent from the country, and Patrick Henry from the convention, but George Washington, Benjamin

Franklin, James Madison, Alexander Hamilton, were present and active. Soon the legislatures of nine different states, led by Delaware and the number completed by New Hampshire, ratified the instrument, and it became the supreme law of the land.

In making this compact, our fathers had before them the example of many ancient and modern attempts at self-government. They were filled with the spirit of personal liberty inherited from the Germanic nations, and especially the Anglo-Saxons and English people; but before their eyes was a living example of a federal republic, which had lived two hundred years, even though surrounded by mighty monarchies hostile to it. From the experience of the united states of the Netherlands they learned, profited, and knew what to avoid. From the Dutch republic, more than from any other model or example, they borrowed much, while the defects of its constitution were avoided or improved upon.

The new government began at Philadelphia, then the central and largest city of the Union. Washington chose Jefferson, Hamilton, Knox, and Randolph to assist him in carrying out his duties as chief executive, and John Jay as head of the Supreme Court. The first three formed what is called the Cabinet. Washington, " the anchor of the Constitution," was a strong Unionist, an American as

"WHY DO YOU DO THAT?" SAID THE PRESIDENT.

against foreigners. He cared nothing about parties. Hamilton, who distrusted a democracy, was a Federalist. He held that a strong national government was the first necessity. Jefferson, who believed ardently in local and state rights, was a Republican-Democrat. It is said that Jefferson preferred only one legislative chamber, as in France. Washington thought there ought to be two, a Senate and House of Representatives. One evening at the supper table, Jefferson, tasting his tea, found it too hot. So he poured it into his saucer.

"Why do you do that?" said the President.

"To let the tea cool," said Jefferson.

"Quite right," said Washington, "and just so we need two legislative chambers to give the judgments of legislators a chance to cool."

The first thing to do was to get money. A duty was levied on all foreign ships and on much of the goods brought to our country. By this revenue tariff the treasury was filled and Hamilton at once began payment of the public debt. We owed Holland and France for money borrowed during the Revolution, and the home debt to our soldiers and civilian creditors was large. The different states were also to be helped in paying what they owed to their citizens. Eight millions were soon disbursed, and the credit of the United States, thus securely founded, has been maintained through all our national history.

The words "mint" and "money" came to us from the Latin, but those of "coin" and "bank" from the Dutch. One of the things most necessary in a new state or an old one is good metal money, that is, coins which everybody, and in every place, will recognize and accept at the value which is stamped upon them. Under the Confederation there were many kinds of paper and pasteboard which passed for money, but very little cash. Usually the money in one state was worth much less in another.

Congress, in 1791, established a United States bank and in 1792 the United States mint. The one supplied paper and the other metallic money which were equally good in all the states.

Hamilton fixed our system of coinage, the simplest and probably the best in the world. Our system is the decimal, based on units of ten, that is, ten mills make a cent, ten cents one dime, ten dimes one dollar, and ten dollars one eagle. This is substantially that of Holland, though with great improvements. Many countries of the world, including even Japan, have followed the American decimal system.

The coinage of the different colonies had been based on that of England, but about the time of the Revolution had become much depreciated. So the Spanish milled dollar was then taken as the standard. On this silver dollar, as on the *pesetas* which one still sees in our country, since the destruction of the Spanish fleet at Santiago, are stamped the Pillars of Hercules with flags or streamers flying. This sign gradually became the dollar mark in American writing. It looks like the letter S with two perpendicular lines drawn through it, thus $. In spite of financial heresies, foolish notions about what money is and the old periodical panics, the wealth and credit of our country have continuously increased. Some day the financial centre of the world will be in New York or Chicago.

Our first census in 1790 showed that we had a population of nearly four millions, who lived on a strip of land about eight leagues wide along the coast of the Atlantic Ocean. Now this little country was in danger of being used by the great European powers for their own selfish purposes. Great Britain wanted to fight her big battles, without much regard to the petty little United States, or any other weak nation. When the British saw American ships carrying supplies to the French, they looked upon it as "blockade-running."

The Scotch-Irish, in western Pennsylvania, did not relish the action of the government in laying taxes upon extracts of rye and wheat. These people, like their fathers in Hibernia and Scotia, were very fond of religion and whiskey. They refused to pay the imposts. They even beat or tarred and feathered the officers sent to collect revenue. One of the first uses of the United States army, under the Constitution, was its despatch by President Washington into western Pennsylvania to put down this first, but not last, manifestation of the liquor power in our country. The troops were mostly Pennsylvanians, and between the Governor's oratory and the presence of the militia the whiskey rebellion, in this primitive form, was soon put down.

From the first Washington set the tone and gave the example of true Americanism. He was for the whole country, and not sections of it. He resisted every attempt of both natives and foreigners to check the growth of real patriotism. The French had risen up against their rulers, beheaded their king, and started a republic. "Citizen Genet" crossed the Atlantic to get American money and ships to help the French fight the English. Many of our people, in their gratitude to France for aid during our Revolution, were more zealous than wise. They rallied round Genet, and it looked as if one half of the Americans would be pro-French and the other half pro-British, and that we should be dragged into a war with England when we were poor, debt-burdened, and least able to defend ourselves. President Washington issued a proclamation of neutrality, which set the American precedent of taking no part in European quarrels.

This showed that the Father of his Country was something else than an English colonial gentleman. He was more, even a true American. Indeed, he was the first to rise above the colonial spirit into the broad idea of a new and grand American nationality. In 1795 he wrote to Patrick Henry: "My ardent desire is to keep the United States free from political connection with every other country, to see them independent of all, and under the influence of none. In a word, I want an American character, that the powers of Europe may be convinced that we act for ourselves and not for others."

Thus this wise and great man, who foresaw our national future, gave us, under God, the true principle of unity. Our fathers listened to his voice, pondered, took "sober second thought," and decided aright and happily for us. Instead of scattering and degenerating, our country began to consolidate and grow. The nation, obeying the true instinct of development, began to expand toward the West. A great stream of population moved over the mountain wall of the Alleghany.

CHAPTER VII.

THE MOVEMENT BEYOND THE ALLEGHANIES.

A MIGHTY line of mountains, called the Appalachian chain, runs southwestwardly from Labrador, and forms the wonderful rock coast of New England, from Maine to Rhode Island. After Narragansett Pier there are no more rocks along the ocean front until we get to South America. Moving inward, the mountain line, by its westward trend, allows a great slope of land between the sea-beach and highlands and from Connecticut to Mississippi. This in the eastern portion is a fertile tide-water region. In the western areas it is rich in grain and pasture lands, grottos and waterfalls, glens and passes. This line makes state boundaries between the Carolinas and Kentucky and Tennessee, furnishing plateaus with some of the most inviting highland soil in the country, and here and there gaps or natural gateways. These allow roads to be built through and over from the east to the west, along which armies, freight and passenger trains can move. Some of them, like Cumberland Gap, are very famous. Through these passes highways were built at state or national expense, and soon great lines of emigration moved over these roads. Various were the forms of vehicle that were built to accommodate the traffic. The famous Conestoga wagon was long and large, with high sides and stout canvas cover, projecting out behind and before. It thus served as a tent, which could be enlarged by opening the side flap. Thousands of families, men, women, and the stronger children, with their faces toward the setting sun, tramped by day and slept on the ground by night. In rainy weather they lived in the wagon, using it as a bedroom at night and kitchen or storehouse by day. Soon villages and towns sprung up, and inns lined the roads.

In the evolution of the nation's system of transportation the Indian trails became first earth roads, with sections of plank or corduroy, then turnpikes, then iron and finally steel railways.

Of all the gaps, that one between Albany and Schenectady, which formed the gateway into the beautiful Mohawk Valley, is the most important, whether for warlike strategy — as military men, from Frontenac in Montreal to Grant on Mount MacGregor, have noticed — or for business. Here the mountains drop down to within a few score feet in height, and a majestic river breaks through the wall of rock at Cohoes and joins the Hudson. At this point of highest value in military strategy was the eastern doorway and end of the Long House of the Six Nations. Through this gap thousands of young and hardy emigrants now poured out from New England to seek more fertile land.

This rush for land was mightily helped by Cupid. Love and enterprise promoted marriage and increased population. Often when a young man would propose to a lady friend or new acquaintance, immediately, should her answer be favorable, both would go to the parson's, be joined in wedlock, and on the same day set out for "the Black River country," or further west. Often, too, the young men and marriageable maidens in the wagon caravans made love and were mated on the way. The church records of marriages at the stopping places, in Schenectady, for example, show how busy the dominies were kept in joining in wedlock young couples who were passing through and westward. Fat were the fees, for youth and hope are generous.

From the Middle States, especially New Jersey, another line of people followed the Indian trails northwestward from Easton, which Sullivan's pioneers had first chopped wide enough to admit the artillery. These two streams from the east, the middle, and the southeast, the Pennsylvania and the Yankee, met at Penn Yan, which they jointly named, each contributing a syllable.

There was no rest in Penn Yan, but onward went the home-seekers further toward the Mississippi and the Pacific.

There was a famous and very popular song, which began:—

> "Oh, of all the mighty nations
> In the East or in the West,
> This glorious Yankee nation
> Is the greatest and the best.
>
> "We have room for all creation,
> And our banner is unfurled,
> Here's a general invitation
> To the people of the world.
>
> *Chorus:* "Come along, come along, make no delay,
> Come from every nation, come from every way,
> Our lands they are broad enough, don't be alarmed,
> For Uncle Sam is rich enough to give us all a farm."

These people streaming westward in the North moved parallel with the grand procession begun by Daniel Boone in the South, which kept increasing. With axe and rifle they crossed Kentucky and Tennessee. Soon in the valleys of the Ohio and Cumberland rose groups of log cabins, cleared spaces in the timber with smiling fields of grain in the bottom lands, and, not very much later, the church spire and the schoolhouse. These showed the beginnings of new states and the promise of the nation's sure expansion, within a few years, to the Mississippi River.

When so much territory was to be occupied, it was highly important that a good system of land measurement and allotment should be formulated. Most of the old soldiers of the Revolution had been paid in land warrants. Many of the veterans sold these warrants for cash, but a large number of the young and strong became actual settlers on their own lands. The greatest danger, as history shows, is, that while every family may and ought to have a certain inheritance and participate in the benefits of landed property, yet sooner or later the soil gets into the hands of a few.

In Europe, in place of the general landholding or common lands of the old Teutonic freemen through ancient times, the Middle Ages brought the tenure of serfs, and the noblemen ruled the country. In England, by a remarkable exception, the land law of the nobles became the land law of the people. In the United States the public lands were a fund for the use of all the people, a source of public revenue and a basis of national finance. They have also served as a means of effecting internal improvements, such as canals, highways, and levees, for the building of great roads and railways, and, best of all, for the promotion of education. As early as 1784 Hamilton and Jefferson initiated measures which laid the foundation of the present system of survey, known as the rectangular system. As Secretary of the Treasury, Hamilton in 1790 furnished the basis of the present method of land administration. It seems curious that the best book in English on "The History of the Land Question in the United States" should be by a Japanese, Shosuke Sato, a fellow of Johns Hopkins University.

It was Simeon De Witt, surveyor general of the State of New York, who first put in practice and carried out the details of that method of land measurement which, borrowed from the Empire State, has come into vogue over the greater part of the United States. Territory is divided into townships of six miles square, the lines running due north and south, with others crossing these at right angles. The townships are subdivided into sections of one mile square, or six hundred and forty acres. Each township contains thirty-six sections, or 23,040 acres. Even when hills, forests, broken or worthless land allow only a partial survey of part of a township, the sections are actually laid out and numbered from south to north and the ranges from east to west.

Simeon De Witt's plan took the place of that one in the Ordinance of 1787 which had "hundreds" or squares of ten geographical miles and lots of one mile square. It is most probable that De Witt's system was imported from Holland and was of Roman origin. After his many years of labors and wanderings were over, De Witt named his own township at the foot of Cayuga Lake, Ulysses, and his place of residence, Ithaca.

It is to be noticed that until 1820 this great mass of emigrants westward were native Americans. They were not Europeans. From 1770 to 1785 there was no emigration from Europe worth speaking of. Until 1820 the number of immigrants averaged only about eight thousand people a year. Land was very cheap, and the terms of sale so liberal that settlers could often pay the price of their farms with the first crops gathered from their newly broken soil. All that a man needed, to get a whole square mile of land, was $331 in cash. The land cost only two dollars an acre. One need only deposit one-twentieth of $1280, which was the price of a section, and then one-fourth of $1280, including deposit, within forty days. The other three-fourths of the whole amount ($960) could be settled for within four years. Fees for application, surveying, etc., amounted to $11.

So began the great American Exodus, properly following the Genesis of the Constitution. Often settlers formed great companies and bought millions of acres, taking up whole townships as fast as the surveyors could locate. They bought on trust, and sold again for wheat, for lumber, or whatever the land would yield. Thus it was that true American settlers, natives of the soil, and not strange foreigners, first cut down our forests, bridged our rivers, and built up towns. In spite of malaria and homesickness, of wild beasts and other "vermin," these stalwart Americans replenished the earth, and laid the foundations for larger advantages to their descendants.

To-day the old virgin forests have disappeared, the beaver dams are forgotten, the trout brooks have narrowed or dried up, and the face of the country is changed almost beyond recognition. Yet the skilled eye can find the site of old leacheries, ash pits, limekilns, lumbermen's camps, and other primitive forest industries, which showed how our grandfathers won their living in a wild country, getting food, money, and prosperity; withal, often wasting, like spendthrifts, the resources of the soil.

In the South the great event of 1793 was the invention of the saw-gin, by Eli Whitney, by which the seed was quickly separated from cotton-wool. Before his time a man could with his fingers and rollers clean about a pound of cotton a day; or, with the Chinese whip and bow, a little more; but Whitney's gin equalled in amount of work done that of three thousand pairs of human hands. The result of this invention was to make the raising of this vegetable wool the most profitable of all crops. Cotton covered hundreds of thousands of acres with snowy balls, riveted slavery upon the southern people, started hundreds of great cotton mills in New England, created a class interested in maintaining slave labor, and, above all, enormously increased our foreign trade. Whereas, in 1784, we had exported only three thousand pounds of cotton, we began within ten years after the invention to export more than forty million pounds. Soon it was said, "cotton is king," for whereas many Asiatic and African countries had been supplying cotton, Americans by their inventive power, added to the peculiar adaptedness of our soil, had won away the culture and trade of the cotton plant so as to make it, for the most part, a distinctively American production. Now we supply not only Europe, but even Japan. Every year the value and demand increase for this wool that grows out of our soil.

But while this Connecticut schoolmaster, sojourning in the South, took the seeds quickly out of cotton, he gave us further seed of long troubles and of civil war, as we shall see. At first the cotton seeds were thrown away as useless refuse. Now, by the application of brain, steam, and machinery, they yield oil, soap, food for cattle, and material for fertilizers. Presto! By the magic of commerce, the reputation of the old countries and the fad for things foreign, cotton-seed oil, after a trip to Europe in bulk, comes back in bottles duly labelled, in Italian, as "olive" oil.

The romance of the conquest by Americans of the forces of nature, for the subduing and replenishing of the earth, is a long story, for which we have not room in this volume. It soon became necessary for Congress to provide a Patent Office, where could be shown models of machines that would work, as well as for the storage of the much larger number that would not.

CHAPTER VIII.

WAR WITH FRANCE ON THE SEA.

WHEN John Adams became President, in 1797, it looked as though we were to have war with France, because the French thought that, having aided us in our struggle against Great Britain, we ought to side with them. Yet Washington had proclaimed neutrality, and most of our fathers were with him. John Adams knew also, very well, as Washington and a majority of the nation, that the motives of the French in helping us had not been like those of the Dutch, — sympathy with our desire for freedom and hope of trade with us, — but that the object was to get possession of Canada and simply to do harm to Great Britain. John Adams had already plainly told Count Vergennes this. Furthermore, the American idea of a republic is something quite different from the French and Spanish-American notion.

The anger of the disappointed French was soon expressed in open hostilities. They not only captured our provision ships and sold them, but they insulted our envoys. Their impudence reached its climax when they demanded money of our government, threatening war in case their bullying claims were not acceded to. The Frenchmen who proposed this bribery were ashamed to come out openly with their own names signed; so they resorted to the coward's device and sent the meanest of all missives — anonymous threatening letters.

The reply of the United States Minister was instant. It was, "No; no; no; not a sixpence." In this he was sustained by the whole American people, whose cry was, "Millions for defence; not one cent for tribute." Mr. C. C. Pinckney, the envoy, had been an officer in the Revolutionary War and a framer of the Constitution. He was ordered to leave France. From this time forth the world learned, as the Barbary powers, and even Great Britain learned, that the United States would never buy a dishonorable peace. Though the Americans love money, they love honor more.

A tremendous wave of excitement rolled over the country. Two new songs were written, "Adams and Liberty," and "Hail, Columbia," which were sung from Maine to Georgia. Washington was again invited to take command of the army which Congress gave power to the President to increase.

In our early history but one department of the government had the oversight of war both on land and sea. By the Act of Congress, April 30, 1798, the navy department was organized separately, so as to be no longer, as before, under the war department. By this time the keels had been laid for six warships, three carrying forty-four, and three thirty-eight guns each. American naval constructors built the *United States*, the *Constitution*, and the *President*, on original models, and these heavy frigates proved to be among the most effective ships in the world. The *Constitution* is the most historic. The *President* was the best and swiftest sailer, and the *United States* was the first vessel to get into the water under the present organization of the navy.

To illustrate the methods of transportation in those days, the sheet copper, with which the *President* was to be sheathed, was rolled at Canton, Massachusetts, and then transported in wagons drawn by oxen that carried the metal to Philadelphia. In that city, at the foot of Swanson Street, she was launched on the 10th of July, 1797.

Of the three thirty-eight-gun ships, the *Chesapeake* was by sailors considered unlucky. The *Constellation* was one of the handsomest of ships. The *Congress* proved to have been one of the oldest and the most useful in the whole navy, when her old age had come.

On the 11th of July, 1798, the new marine corps was established by law, in place of the old one. Five days later, in the same year, it was voted that the navy of the United States should consist of thirty active cruisers. About the same time Congress by law denounced all the treaties with France, because the French had begun depredations upon our commerce and made themselves our enemy. As war was looming up, Captain Richard Dale, in the *Ganges*,—the first man-of-war to get to sea under the new navy department,—was ordered to capture French cruisers on our coast or to recapture their prizes. At this time the new frigates were not ready, for our country was then very deficient in guns, naval stores, and spars.

When the *Constellation* was able to get to sea, she was put under the command of Captain Thomas Truxton. The first vessel made a prize of by our navy was taken by the United States sloop of war *Delaware*, commanded by Captain Decatur, who captured the French privateer *Le Croyable*. The name of the prize was changed into the *Retaliation*, and she was put under command of Lieutenant Bainbridge. Pretty soon the frigate *United States*, under Captain Barry, got to sea.

Now began the real education of our officers and the deposit of those traditions which are a part of the life of the service. There was no naval academy then, except on the ship's deck, and our great commanders often began as boys of twelve. The *Constitution*, under Captain Samuel Nicholson, was also in commission by July 20, 1797. Then our war-ships convoyed fleets of our merchantmen safely between the West Indies and our northern ports. By the end of 1798 we had twenty-three ships of war afloat. The programme of naval enlargement became so popular that several national ships were built by subscription in different cities and presented to the government.

The *Retaliation* did not have a long career under the American flag. She was captured by two French frigates, and thus both sides, French and American, had made captures and come out even. By the opening of the year 1799 we had twenty-eight war-ships afloat. Now came the time to test the merits of the new American heavy frigate, for this craft was of a novel type. Americans have always led the way in naval designs.

When, on the 9th of February, Commodore Truxton in the *Constellation*, with a brave and eager crew, fell in with the French frigate *Insurgente*, the first heavy naval combat since the Revolution began. The *Constellation* suffered first the loss of her foretop mast, but after several broadsides got where she could rake the enemy. After firing three broadsides through and along the hull of her enemy, she shot out of the smoke, wore round and was again ready with all her guns loaded to rake the *Insurgente* from stern to stem.

The French captain, after a loss of seventy men, seeing his peril, struck his flag at 3.30 P.M., and the one hour's battle ended.

The *Constellation* had but three men wounded. One man was run through by his own officer, for having flinched at his gun. The law of the battle-deck does not allow of cowardice, lest by the default of one the whole crew should be panic-stricken, and defeat be made certain. Years before, in the attack on Stony Point, one of Wayne's men suffered death at the hands of an officer and in the same way. This was for turning aside to load his musket when the general had ordered empty guns and cold steel.

The first lieutenant of the *Constellation*, John Rodgers, afterward commodore, was put on board the *Insurgente* with eleven men to take the prize to St. Kitts in the West Indies. There were still 173 of the French crew on board when it began to blow, and darkness coming on the work of transferring the prisoners had to stop and the two ships separated in the darkness. With the decks still covered with the wreck of sails, spars, rigging, and splintered timber left by the battle, dead and wounded lying about and their blood running out of the scuppers, and the prisoners expecting to rise and recapture their ship, Rodgers's situation was awkward indeed. He kept the Frenchmen below and set armed sentinels during the three days. He finally brought the *Insurgente* to St. Kitts, meeting the *Constellation* already there.

This victory awakened tremendous popularity in favor of our navy. Lads and sailors pressed forward to enlist, and the young men of our best families were only too glad to get commissions as midshipmen. The government began a career of well-planned naval expansion. Captain Preble convoyed American vessels to the Dutch East Indies. Then the stars and stripes were first seen on an American man-of-war east of the Cape of Good Hope. France having taken Holland, and being at war with England, the annual Dutch ship from Batavia to Nagasaki could not sail under Dutch colors. So the American Captain Stewart took her to Nagasaki under our flag, and for the first time the sixteen stars and thirteen stripes were mirrored on the Black Tide of Japan. The people in the land of Tycoon and Mikado were much interested in the " flowery flag."

Congress persevered in the work of building up a superb marine, and even six 74-gun ships were contracted for. It may be truly said that at the opening of the nineteenth century the navy made as brilliant a record as it has done at its close. The six heavy frigates were afloat, and there were altogether in the West India waters or nearer home twenty-five men-of-war, one of them being the old *Insurgente* refitted. The cruising fleet was divided into two squadrons, one under Commodore Talbot, who had ten, and the other under Commodore Truxton, who had as many more. Nevertheless the seas were swarming with Gallic cruisers and privateers, and our commerce suffered. This was the era of the French "Spoliations." I could tell many "tales of a grandfather" who had experience of capture and loss.

On the 1st of February, 1800, Commodore Truxton, in the *Constellation*, fell in with the French frigate, *Vengeance*, with fifty-two guns and five hundred men. Putting on all sail, Truxton came up to hail the Frenchman, when the latter opened fire from his stern and port guns. A battle began which lasted from eight o'clock in the evening until one o'clock in the morning. Then the French ship, having lost one hundred and fifty men killed and wounded, drew off. The *Constellation*, losing her main mast, which went overboard, was unable to make chase. The *Vengeance* got into Curaçoa dismasted and in a sinking condition. This battle added tremendously to the reputation of Truxton and our navy.

Another brilliant action was the capture of a French privateer, the *Sandwich*, formerly of English ownership, at Port Platte, by a party of seamen and marines in the sloop *Sally*, led by Lieutenant Hull of the *Constitution*, who afterward commanded this famous ship. Later the *Insurgente* sailed on a cruise. She must have foundered at sea, for nothing was ever heard of her. This made the fourth ship of the American navy lost in this way. There were a good many minor conflicts at sea and captures of French privateers by our vessels during this naval war with France. Nevertheless Napoleon Bonaparte saw that there was no real ground of hostilities between the two nations that had lately been allies. Overthrowing the government at Paris, he became first consul and proposed peace. On the 3d of February, 1801, the treaty of amity with France was ratified by the Senate, and a man-of-war, well named the *Herald*, was sent to the West Indies to recall all our armed ships.

Thus ended this short and irregular war with France, in which our naval officers were trained to enterprise and action. This campaign was only the prelude to the splendid naval drama on the Mediterranean.

No one saw more clearly than Napoleon the future of the American people. No one believed more surely in the time, not far away, when the United States should first be the commercial rival and then the superior of Great Britain. It is no wonder, then, that as soon as this " man of destiny" came in power, he made peace with the United States. Furthermore, he was soon ready to sell out all French claims to territory in America. And so, to this Corsican dictator we owe it that our territory was doubled and our country began the policy of continued national expansion. When Washington died, in 1799, Bonaparte ordered public mourning for him in France, though the British also lowered their flags to half mast. Our war with France was the first war under the new Constitution.

CHAPTER IX.

OUR NAVY IN THE MEDITERRANEAN.

WHILE our country was so young and weak, it had not yet made its flag respected on the high seas, and especially in the Mediterranean Sea. A line of robber nations, from Egypt to the Atlantic Ocean, held North Africa and dominated the seacoast. These Barbary states were Tunis, Tripoli, Morocco, and Algiers. The pirates were Mohammedans, and thought they were doing God service in robbing Christian ships, making their crews prisoners, and then holding them as slaves or for ransom. They had heavily armed, fast sailing vessels, called corsairs, which swooped like hawks upon their prey. Thus they grew rich on their villanous work. Even strong European nations had to bribe these fanatical robbers. Our government paid the Dey of Tripoli many thousand dollars a year to allow our ships to pass his coast. Having no navy, we could not fight or defend ourselves.

These Barbary powers at first, during the Middle Ages, had carried on this naval warfare for what they called religion. Then finding such "religion" very profitable, they kept it up, for both their conscience' and pocket's sake. Before the Revolution, our annual trade in the Mediterranean, which amounted to twenty thousand tons a year, was protected by passes from the British government at London. After our independence was gained our young and weak nation had to guard against these new enemies — the piratical Moors.

As in 1898, so in 1785, it was "the Maine" that began the war. A schooner of that name was captured by the Dey of Algiers and her crew imprisoned as slaves. Other captures followed. In 1792 Washington proposed a treaty with Algiers, which was to pay $40,000 as a ransom for the thirteen Americans then held captive, $25,000 as a present to the Dey on putting his signature to the treaty, and $25,000 a year annually. Admiral Paul Jones was given charge of the negotiations, but unfortunately he died at this time. Soon after this the Algerine fleet captured ten of our vessels, and in November, 1793, there were one hundred and fifteen American prisoners in Algiers alone. Yet, although our fellow-countrymen had been seized and worked in chain gangs as slaves, our country, instead of punishing the rascals, kept bleating like a fat sheep. The government had to ask the churches and Christian people to take up collections during hours of worship, to raise money to pay ransoms. Meanwhile the proud thieves became more insolent and demanded more.

The firing of salutes is the wasteful etiquette observed between ships of different nations and recognition of officers of high rank. It costs more every year to burn powder thus foolishly than it does to support Christian missionaries all over the world. In 1797 it was proposed, on the side of the Bey of Tunis, that a barrel of gunpowder should be given the Tunisian government for every gun fired in saluting an American ship of war. To this our envoy Barlow objected, though the Bey insisted upon it, because, he said, "fifteen barrels of gunpowder will furnish a cruiser, which may capture a prize and net me a hundred thousand dollars." The consul replied that "the concession was so degrading that our nation would not yield to it,— both justice and honor forbade,— and we did not doubt the world would view the demand as they did the concession." "You consult your honor," said he; "I my interest; but if you wish to save your honor in this instance, give me fifty barrels of powder annually and I will agree to the alteration." This treaty with Tunis cost us $107,000, and up to 1802 our diplomacy with these marauders amounted to over $2,000,000 — enough to have built twenty large frigates. Indeed, half of this amount, properly invested in good American men-of-war and the pay of our brave sailors, would have saved us the degradation of handing over bribery money during many years, for then we should have had peace, without paying a single dollar for either tribute or ransom.

As matter of fact our treaties with the Barbary nations amounted to nothing until we sent a naval force into the Mediterranean. For each one of the Mohammedan robbers demanded as much money as the others did, and during all the negotiations the United States were put on a level with Sweden. The more the barbarians were paid, the more they wanted.

Mr. William Eaton, United States Consul at Tunis, accompanied our first squadron of four vessels and was presented to the Dey. He thus describes that ruler's private audience room, twelve by eight feet in size: "Here [in the narrow dark entry, leading to the room] we took off our shoes and entering the cave (for so it seemed) with small apertures of light, with iron gates, we were shown to a large, huge, shaggy beast, sitting on his rump upon a low bench, covered with a cushion of embroidered velvet, with his hind legs gathered up like a tailor or a bear. On our approach to him he reached out his forepaw as if to receive something to eat. Our guide exclaimed 'kiss the Dey's hand!' The Consul-General bowed very elegantly and kissed it, and we followed his example in succession. The animal seemed at that moment to be in a harmless mood; he grinned several times, but made very little noise. After standing a few moments in silent agony, the American company left the den, without any other hindrance than the humiliation of being obliged, in this involuntary manner, to violate the second command of God and offend common decency."

The little American frigate *George Washington* was in the harbor of Algiers in October, 1800, when the Dey demanded of the American Consul the privilege of using this vessel to carry his ambassador to the port of Constantinople, with the customary presents. He threatened war, plunder, and devastation unless his demands were satisfied. So weak and low had we become in the eyes of these barbarians, that the captain of the *George Washington* had to hoist the flag of Algiers at the main top and salute it with seven guns. However, this little war vessel, which went to Constantinople, was the first to show the American flag in the Bosphorus, and thus the thirteen stripes and sixteen stars were reflected on the waters of eastern Europe.

Yet no benefit came from our degradation. The Dey was a sharp bargain maker, declaring that the naval stores were not up to the mark. Instead of reckoning by the Christian calendar, he computed according to the Mohammedan years, and by the year 1812 found our government deficient to the amount of $27,000, by which time we had paid about $379,000.

When the Bashaw of Tripoli found that the United States government had bribed the Dey of Algiers at a higher price than himself, he behaved like a dissatisfied small boy. This Oriental Oliver Twist clamored for more presents and money. These not coming when expected, he cut down the flagstaff of the American Consulate May 14, 1801, and began war.

Finally our government took measures to protect American citizens even beyond the ocean. Captain Dale was sent with the three frigates, *President*, *Philadelphia*, and *Essex*, and the gunboat *Enterprise*. These arrived at Gibraltar in time to keep two Tripolitan ships of war from getting into the Atlantic Ocean to prey on our commerce. The presence of our navy had more influence in maintaining peace than if the frigate *George Washington* had come again laden with tribute.

The first trial of prowess between the Turks and Americans was when the *Enterprise* fell in with a Tripolitan corsair, then out on a predatory cruise. The Turk, after fighting a while, struck his flag but hoisted it again, thinking to gain an advantage.

After three hours' battle, the American fire had been so destructive that the Turkish captain threw his colors into the sea, and asked for quarter. Fifty men on the pirate ship had been killed or wounded, while on the *Enterprise* was not a man hurt. Our men first attended to the wounded, and then threw the Turks' guns overboard, gave the ship a sail and spar, and allowed the crew to go back to Tripoli. Yet the Tripolitan captain's bravery, and even his wounds, did not avail with the Dey. He was placed on a jackass, ridden through the streets, and then given the bastinado.

Our vessels blockaded Tripoli and kept the corsairs from coming out, but the Dey, caring nothing for his own people, would exchange no prisoners. He still held the American captives, hoping for large ransom. In 1802 another fine squadron, under Commodore Morris, kept up the blockade, but little was accomplished, and the Moors kept up their piratical activity. On August 26, 1803, the *Philadelphia* captured the *Meshboha*, belonging to the Emperor of Morocco, but, on October 31st, while chasing a Tripolitan vessel, ran hard and high upon the rocks, where she was wedged fast. Though everything was done to lighten her, the ship could not be got off. No other American vessel was near to help, and under the attack of nine gunboats our flag was hauled down. The Americans were robbed and plundered, and Captain Bainbridge and his men were thrown into prison. The Divan was highly elated and expected large ransom. Things looked dark for the Americans.

Commodore Preble, one of the first and greatest educators of the United States navy, was put in command of the American forces in the Mediterranean. To prevent the *Philadelphia* from being refitted as a piratical corsair, Decatur, with brave officers and a picked crew of seventy men, boldly planned to run in at night and set the frigate on fire.

This scheme was carried out on a moonlight night. Our men lay concealed on the ketch *Intrepid*, and the Turks, thinking the boat was a Maltese trading vessel, were completely surprised. Decatur sprang on board, leading his men. They cleared the spar deck by driving the Turks into the sea, and won complete victory after a struggle below. Then the combustibles were passed up, the ship set on fire in a dozen places, and soon masts and rigging made glowing columns and capitals of fire. Indeed, the Americans themselves barely escaped from the flames. The spirit of the United States navy rose high, and our merchant vessels, in consequence of the general war then prevailing in Europe, began again to " whiten the seas of the Old World with American commerce."

On August 3, 1804, Commodore Preble, with 7 men-of-war, 2 bomb-vessels, and 6 gunboats manned by 1060 men, bombarded the forts and fought the enemy's war-ships. In the harbor were 115 cannon mounted in battery, 19 gunboats, and 5 men-of-war. Besides the science and skill shown by Preble, his officers, Decatur, Somers, Trippe, Bainbridge, Thorne, McDonough, Henley, Ridley, and Miller, won fame and distinction, while the *Constitution* revealed her splendid qualities both as a sailer and a floating fortress. There were hand-to-hand fights, and 2 boats were captured by Decatur, which had on board 80 men, of whom 52 were killed or wounded. With 11 Americans, Lieutenant Trippe boarded and captured another vessel having a crew thrice as large in number as his own.

Several points were made prominent in this battle: first, the superiority of the American gunnery, and, second, the courage and effectiveness of our men in boarding. The muscular Mussulmans had always supposed that they excelled and were invincible with the pike and cimeter. Besides the three gunboats taken, three more were sunk, and the batteries were badly damaged.

Other bombardments followed, but we had no land forces to reduce the fortified city, and the Dey still insisted on a ransom of $500 apiece for his prisoners.

In the old naval warfare, and until well into the present century, great reliance was placed upon fire-ships, or floating mines, for submarine mines were at that time unknown. Captain Somers offered to take in a bomb-ketch close to the shipping and batteries and blow them up. The *Intrepid* was loaded with powder and combustibles, and called an "infernal," and great things were expected of this "hell-burner." But although manned by brave and cool men, the *Intrepid* blew up prematurely, and all on board perished. Whether by shots from the enemy, or by accident, or to avoid capture, is unknown, for no one survived to tell how or why. "A sad and solemn mystery, after all our conjectures, must forever veil the fate of these fearless officers and their hardy followers."

The name of Somers became a battle-cry, and has been given to our ships of war. Had the *Intrepid* succeeded, there would have been peace within twenty-four hours; but since it failed, the barbarian ruler still hoped that the Americans would submit to capture and give ransom, rather than pay money for a navy so far from home. On the contrary, our squadron was kept up.

Then came the affair of General Eaton, who, with a motley force, captured Derne, and the treaty of 1805, which was of no special credit to our government. As a naval campaign, the war in the Mediterranean was, in its results, at least respectable; while as a school for the forming and education of the United States navy, these four years of experience in the Mediterranean were of incalculable value, and later we shall see good results.

CHAPTER X.

DOUBLING THE NATIONAL DOMAIN.

AMERICAN diplomacy really began with the mission of Franklin to France in 1776. Other envoys were despatched, such as John Adams, Silas Deane, and Henry Laurens. Dr. Franklin, by his wit and wisdom, by his eminence in science and philosophy, and by his unique and commanding personality, which attracted the attention of the Bourbon court, and especially of the elegant ladies of Paris and Versailles, made a signal success. He obtained from the French money, ships, an army, and loans, besides commissioning privateers and securing the services of John Paul Jones. One of the pleasant surprises to the American visiting France is to see so often the portraits of " Poor Richard."

John Adams was successful, especially in Holland, where he secured recognition of the United States and loans of money. These, when paid up in 1829, amounted in principal and interest to $14,000,000. While our various American envoys were in Europe, much real sympathy with our country was awakened. Not a few Frenchmen and Dutchmen made real personal sacrifices in behalf of American freedom; but in the great flock of European adventurers that offered to serve in our cause, and to accept commissions in the army, many were worthless characters. Not a few duels were fought between French and American officers, for our men could not stand the aristocratic airs of these supercilious servants of the Bourbon and other monarchies. Congress was only too ready to commission these soldiers of fortune whom Silas Deane recommended; but Washington did not like the policy of employing many foreigners. He wrote that if our liberties were to be achieved, the war must be fought and the victories won by Americans if at all. As for Spain, we got no help from her as an ally, and it was well for us that we did not. The one European people that from first to last really sympathized with us were the Dutch, whose history was so much like our own.

Our national diplomacy under the Constitution began when John Jay was sent by Washington, in 1795, to make a new treaty, because the treaty of 1783 had not been carried out properly by either party, British or American. Our people did not keep their word and pay their debts. On the other hand, the British government, besides hampering our trade with France, kept the Indians in hostility

to us, and would not give up the forts along the
northern frontier, as had been promised. The
treaty which John Jay secured was very unpopular
with our grandfathers, who were greedy enough in
wanting to get more than they really deserved; while
on their part the British tried to use us as their
unwilling ally against France, and interfered unlawfully with our commerce.

By the Jay treaty the eastern boundary of Maine
was settled, our citizens recovered about $10,000,000
for illegal captures by British ships of war, and
the western forts held by British garrisons were
surrendered to us. This was all very fine for
our side, but to offset these advantages our trading
ships were shut out from Canadian ports, and placed
under restrictions in the West Indies, while nothing
was said about impressing our sailors in the British
navy, nor anything about neutrality, as between the
French and British privateers, for the British government refused to settle these matters.

So a tremendous excitement ensued. Public
meetings were held denouncing Washington. At
Boston, Jay was burned in effigy, but was nevertheless made Governor of New York for six years, and
under his auspices slavery was abolished in the
Empire State. Washington approved the treaty,
because he thought it was the best which we could
at that time obtain; for weak nations could not

then, and perhaps cannot now, be treated on equal terms with more powerful nations. Our country was puny, but alive and growing, and unable as yet to compel the respect of the great nations of Europe, then in conflict with each other. The War of 1812, which on the ocean gathered in for our heroes a sheaf of British flags, was necessary to compel Great Britain to respect us. No one more than an Englishman respects you when you beat him in a fair fight.

When Jefferson became President, the capital had been removed from Philadelphia to Washington, which was then a little village in the midst of a ten-mile tract of land covered with woods. Instead of being built to face the future and the splendid city of to-day, the façade of the capital confronted a little straggling village where the "old families" were supposed to live.

The idea of having a capital in a district which had no vote in Congress, and in which no individual could vote, in either state or national elections, without going home to his birthplace or residence, was borrowed from the Hague in the Dutch republic. Washington and Adams, who were the stadholders, that is, holders of power in place of American people, had imitated a little the manners and ceremonies of kings. President Washington had, especially, put on great state and dignity both at official receptions and at social balls, and in attending and going from church. The "Republican Court" was a scene of great splendor and dignity.

As I have heard my grandmother and grand-aunts tell, President Washington would be driven in a coach and six horses to Old Christ Church, on Second Street, above Market, in Philadelphia. Dressed in black velvet, waited upon by his obsequious lackeys and footmen, and driven by Fritz, his famous Hessian coachman, he made a great show of pomp and splendor, which not only the boys and girls, but the ladies and gentlemen of the capital city, delighted in viewing.

Jefferson, who had democratic ideas that emerged during the French Revolution, dressed more plainly and cared little for display, while at the same time fashions were tending toward the simpler style of to-day. Besides the great change from silk waistcoat, lace ruffs and wristlets, knee-breeches, silk stockings and silver buckles, men were beginning to wear trousers, and their coats and hats were more like those of our time. Jefferson carried his simpler manners and habits to the capital and in the executive mansion. This was not the present White House, but one which had been occupied by President Adams, and which was burned by the British in 1814.

It was under Jefferson that the great expansion

programme, now over a century old and yet unfinished, began to be carried out. A study of the facts shows that the thoughts of Americans " widened with the process of the suns." In colonial days a road had been made from Plymouth, nine miles westward, which there stopped, it not being then supposed that any regular travel further westward would ever be needed. In 1690 the village of Schenectady was spoken of as " in the far West." A hundred years later the removal of the capital to Washington was opposed as being " too far toward the setting sun." In Jefferson's time many able men shook their heads at the idea of the republic extending beyond the Alleghanies. Many also supposed that in time the different sections would break up into nations. Indeed, it is no wonder that good and wise men held these views, for then it took more time to go from Baltimore to Pittsburg than is now required to reach Europe, or to travel from California to Hawaii. From San Francisco one can reach the Philippines more easily and more quickly, than even the swiftest and bravest hunter could get from Philadelphia to the Mississippi River.

Yet even while men were thus thinking and talking, the very ones who believed in having a country no wider than two hundred and fifty miles were staggered with the proposition to buy the very heart of the American continent, between the Mississippi

River and the Rocky Mountains. France owned this territory called Louisiana, named by La Salle, its discoverer, after Louis XIV and his queen. Instead of being the district still retaining the name, it extended from the Gulf of Mexico to Canada. Out of this vast region watered by the Red, the Arkansas, and the Missouri rivers and their tributaries, over a dozen states and territories have been made.

Napoleon Bonaparte had determined on ruling, if possible, all Europe, and on bringing even Great Britain under subjugation. For this gigantic task he needed plenty of money. Moreover, he feared the capture of Louisiana by the British fleet. So when the offer to sell was made, Mr. Jefferson, though not liking the idea of national enlargement, and stretching his constitutional power, as he himself confessed, "till it cracked," bought a million square miles, or over six hundred millions of acres, at two and a half cents an acre, and Napoleon got $15,000,000. Thus all possible disputes with France were removed out of politics; England would never control the Mississippi Valley; the great West became ours and opened to our settlers. The grandest river and valley on the continent, with the precious jewel of the Crescent City, came under the American flag, then glistening with seventeen stars. Our national domain was doubled.

CHAPTER XI.

WHY A SECOND WAR FOR FREEDOM WAS FOUGHT.

JEFFERSON'S plan of defending our Atlantic coast by a flotilla of little gunboats seems very amusing to-day when we think of the proud and powerful nations of France and Great Britain. These were then at war, and in their fighting they cared very little about the rights of smaller countries. Each went so far as to forbid Americans to trade with the other. Great Britain demanded the right to stop our ships and search them, in order to get British sailors. Every man who could not prove his American citizenship was dragged away and forced to enter the British service.

The success of the British, especially after Nelson's victories and Trafalgar, had transformed many English captains into genuine bullies. Indeed, this is the usual effect of most successful wars, — to fill the victors with inordinate pride, — and it is one reason why war ought to cease from the earth. Several thousand men were taken off our ships in this way, and things seemed to be going on from bad to worse, when an event took place through which

Providence taught our country and the American navy a bitter, but a very wholesome, lesson. It was the first and the last time that an American man-of-war was fired on without response.

The United States frigate *Chesapeake* had sailed for Hampton Roads, and was hailed by a British war vessel *Leopard*. Officers came on board to muster the *Chesapeake's* crew, to see if there were any of their sailors on board. This Commodore Barron refused to permit, or to allow his men to be mustered by any except their own officers. Noticing that the decks were littered up and the ship utterly unprepared, the British lieutenant returned in his boat to the *Leopard*. In a few minutes the British trained her guns and opened fire upon the *Chesapeake*. This was in time of peace and without provocation, for Commodore Barron had written a letter stating that he knew of no British deserters on his ship. Utterly unprepared, no reply with fire and shot to the treacherous bully could be made. The *Chesapeake's* crew were so unready that even the single cannon discharged was fired by an officer who carried in his hands a live coal from the cook's galley and placed it upon the powder of the touch-hole. The *Chesapeake* struck her colors, and the British took off three men, but let Commodore Barron return to Norfolk with his ship.

Yet the moral effect of this affair was excellent,

and the ultimate benefit to the Americans very great. Very little damage had been done by the British cannon balls. The mist of rumor and exaggeration of the power of the British broadside were blown away, and for all time our navy learned the lesson of being always ready and effective. Now, no ships are neater, no crews are more vigilant, and no officers are in more constant preparation for the possibilities of action, whether the time be one of war or peace, than are those of the United States.

But instead of going on to increase and perfect our navy, Congress foolishly passed laws called the Embargo and Non-intercourse acts, which forbade any American vessels sailing from our ports. By paralyzing our commerce, it was hoped that France and England would behave themselves. This was like cutting off one's own arm to make men respect you, instead of using it for defence. We lost time, trade, money, and ships.

Nevertheless one good result sprang out of this suicidal policy. The stream of American energy, turned back by this dam, found outlet in another direction. Factories rose, and soon new wheels were turning. The New Englanders turned their attention to manufactures and labor-saving inventions. The Pennsylvanian, Fulton, launched his steamboat on the Hudson, and the *Clermont* moved without wind or oars against wind and current from

New York to Albany. The puffing monster scared some of the farmers, who thought that the devil was riding up the river on a sawmill. The fishermen and sailors were awed almost as much as the Indians had been, two centuries before, by Henry Hudson and his ship *Half Moon*. In the far Northwest Lewis and Clarke explored the Missouri River valley beyond the Rocky Mountains and down the Columbia River, which was first named after his own vessel, by Captain Robert Gray, who carried the American flag around the world. Soon steamboats began carrying emigrants and stimulating traffic on the Ohio, the Mississippi, the western rivers, and the Great Lakes. A few years later the first ocean steamer crossed from Savannah to Europe, bearing the American flag.

When James Madison, often called "the Father of the Constitution," was chosen President and came into office, thousands of American ships were rotting at their wharves. Their owners waited impatiently for the liberty of commerce. Misled by what the British minister at Washington had promised, that they would be unmolested by British men-of-war if they traded only in English ports, they started out on the ocean, turning the cold shoulder to France. But American captains soon found that England would not cease searching our ships, nor did Napoleon keep his word any better. When, further, as was believed, British agents stirred up Tecumseh, an Indian chief of Ohio, who united the savage clans from Florida to Michigan to break up the white settlements, General William Henry Harrison marched into Indiana. At Tippecanoe, in 1811, he defeated the embattled redmen.

Other incidents came to aggravate the bitter feelings between the United States and Great Britain. Commodore John Rodgers and other naval captains believed that our men and ships could meet the British on the seas with fair prospect of success. Having confidence in the merits of the American long gun and the heavy frigate, they determined to leave nothing to chance. They constantly drilled their men both at cannon and carronades, and with cutlass, pike, and pistol. They determined, when they got a chance, to put an end to the abominable habit of the searching of our ships by the heroes of Trafalgar, whom long success had made insolent.

Gradually a party was formed in this country which had representatives in Congress, whose creed was that war with Great Britain would consolidate the union of the states, and thus benefit the country by developing its resources. The cry went up for "free trade and sailors' rights." This meant freedom to trade with any country that would trade with us, and protection of American seamen against seizure.

Naval fashions of that day called for a vast area of canvas on the sailing ships, with enormous flags and streamers. One British vessel, the *Guerrière*, had her name painted in large letters on the topsails. Captain Dacres, her commander, had become conspicuous for his bravado in insulting American merchant captains. Since 1790 a question of impressment, or the press gang, had been debated between Washington and London, without much apparent benefit; but now Commodore Rodgers received orders to put an end to these outrages, which made such annoying delay and greatly injured trade. Burning to revenge the *Chesapeake* affair, the frigate *President* put to sea with her name boldly blazoned on her three topsails like those of the *Guerrière*.

When near Sandy Hook an episode took place which precipitated the War of 1812. At half-past eight in the evening of May 17th, Commodore Rodgers signalled a strange sail, asking, "What ship is that?" The hailed vessel replied with four cannon shot. Then began a general fusillade, which lasted fifteen minutes. The British sloop of war, *Little Bell*, had foolishly attacked an American heavy frigate. The next morning it was found that the smaller vessel, though terribly shattered, was able to proceed on her course. The accounts of the affair given by the two commanders cannot be reconciled, but the breach was widened. Although it was, and always will be, a disgrace to their Christianity for English-speaking people to shed each other's blood, war broke out.

When hostilities began the British had over a thousand armed ships. Flushed with their victories under Lord Nelson, and excited by the sea songs of Dibdin, they considered themselves "lords of the main." In their naval battles they had sunk hundreds of French ships, many of them as large and heavy as their own, and they had won flags French, Dutch, Spanish, Danish, by the hundreds. No one can ever accuse the British sailors or soldiers of a lack of courage. Now, however, they were to learn from their own kinsmen that brute force is less valuable in war than intelligence, and that a little navy, contemptible in size, could strike down more British flags in a generation than they had lost in a century.

On the American side were a few first-class ships and excellent guns manned and served mainly by native Americans. Although Congress had neglected the navy, yet Commodore Rodgers's squadron was in the finest condition. As a rule, the British navy had no ships equal in general effectiveness to the American heavy frigates, the long guns of which had sights fitted to them, which enabled our men to fire with wonderful accuracy.

In using sheet-lead cartridges, they anticipated the copper shells of later American invention. Furthermore, our men were drilled to be cool and to wait until the exact moment of firing. The Americans took more care of their guns, fastened them more securely, did not overload them, counted rather than weighed their shot, and depended on intelligence rather than on numbers. Besides the long guns were the short and chubby carronades, named from the Carron iron works in Scotland, where they were first made. These did terrible execution at close range in tearing up sails, rigging, and thus disabling the enemy.

The naval officer of the early part of our century was usually a handsome man, with a sufficient number of gilt buttons and expanse of gold braid on his coat to make him greatly admired of the ladies. The old pigtail and eelskin of the Revolutionary days had passed away at the dictate of fashion. Most of the officers had more or less wavy hair. How so many of them were able to make their hair curl is a mystery, but there is no secret as to why none of them wore mustaches or beards, for these things were not in fashion. Even individuals, however eminent on deck or in port, could not gratify their taste, had they desired to keep the upper lip covered; for the regulations of the navy forbade the growth of hair on the face or chin, and would not tolerate a mustache "under any circumstances." So in their portraits we see the epauletted naval heroes with high stocks and stand-up collars, with ruffled shirt bosoms, but only "sides" or short columns of whiskers below their ears, or occasionally coming forward toward the mouth or high up on the cheek.

One great difference in the general spirit of the navy and that of the army in 1812, as in 1898, lay in this, that the navy was a purely professional school, in which only trained men thoroughly equipped for their work took part. Patriotism had thus the best chance to show itself. On the contrary, the army, except the small nucleus of the regulars, became the prey of partisan politicians and of men ignorant of the scientific work of the true soldier. The navy had a further advantage in that the Tripolitan war had been a magnificent training-school for our officers. Commodore Preble was really the father of the American navy, for he infused in it his dauntless spirit, and made the young officers proud of their calling. Under his own eyes were trained Hull, Decatur, Bainbridge, McDonough, Porter, Lawrence, Biddle, Chauncey, Warrington, Charles Morris, and Stewart, all of whom, in 1812, kept our flag afloat on the seas, and won fame in the war with the mightiest naval power on this planet.

CHAPTER XII.

THE NAVAL CAMPAIGN OF 1812.

WHEN the declaration of war was made by Congress on the 12th of June, 1812, there was no money in the treasury and the Cabinet was divided. On our side some of the veterans of the Revolution were living. So also was King George III. So great was the cowardly fear of British invincibility on the seas, that some in Washington urged that our men-of-war should keep within tidewater, and act only as harbor batteries. We had then only three first-class and two second-class frigates which were seaworthy, together with five brigs and sloops and three second-class frigates under repair, besides the one hundred and seventy little gunboats. Captains Bainbridge and Stewart went in person to remonstrate against the frigates being kept at home. Commodore Rodgers, as soon as news of the declaration of war came, moved out to sea, so as not to receive orders of recall. He was in charge of the *President, United States, Congress, Argus,* and *Hornet*—one-third of our whole naval force at that time.

The naval campaign of 1812–1815 was one of the most wonderful in the annals of ocean war. Within two years the British lost more flags, through capture by Americans, than had been won from them by their foes during the previous two centuries. The first gun afloat was fired by Commodore John Rodgers, who, in the *President*, the best sailing ship of the navy, chased the *Belvidere*, which, however, escaped to Halifax. Then, crossing the ocean, Rodgers wrought great havoc on the British commerce off the Norway coast and in the seas around Great Britain. It was found necessary in London to despatch a great fleet of ships to find Rodgers, who, however, came back safely. Soon the Admiralty in London issued an order to their war vessels to refuse battle with the Americans, except upon rigidly equal terms. They called our heavy frigates "disguised seventy-fours."

The first combat at sea struck the keynote of victory. Captain Isaac Hull, in the *Constitution*, was chased by three British frigates, but surprised his veteran opponents by his bold and original methods of seamanship, and got off safely. Later, in the Gulf of St. Lawrence, he met alone and by herself the British man-of-war *Guerrière*, one of his late pursuers. This vessel had been captured from the French, and its name was only another form of the word "warrior." Then began the first of fifteen naval battles, twelve of which were won by Americans.

The *Guerrière* moved gayly to the work of battle and began firing rapidly, but Captain Hull kept his officers and men waiting until the right moment. They found it very hard to stand still, all expectant and excited as they were, and be fired at without making reply; but, when once the 24-pounders began their music, so welcome to the ears of our tars, only twenty minutes were necessary to reduce the British ship to firewood. Every one of the masts of the *Guerrière* was shot away, and her hull was so badly smashed by the American 24-pounders that she drifted helplessly as a hulk and had to be set on fire. When Captain Hull came into Boston with his prisoners, the ship, almost uninjured, was dubbed *Old Ironsides*.

In October, 1812, Captain Jacob Jones in the sloop *Wasp* met his Britannic Majesty's brig *Frolic* and gave battle, which began in a rough sea. Both ships had about the same force of men and guns, but British sailors seemed to blaze away without taking much aim, while the American artillerists always pointed their guns. The *Frolic* fired as she rose on the wave, the *Wasp* fired as she sunk, and every shot seemed to tell on the hull of her antagonist. The consequences were that the comparative loss of the British and the Americans in this naval duel, as in that of the *Constitution* and *Guerrière*, was five to one. Soon after the combat the British seventy-four-gun ship *Poictiers* appeared and took both the *Wasp* and the *Frolic*.

This was in substance a civil war, for English-speaking men, with much the same ideas, were fighting each other and were equally brave; but our ships were the best built in the world, and in nearly every case the Americans had the advantages in throwing heavier shot and often having more guns in a broadside. Yet even these facts do not account for the tremendous victories gained. The true reason was that the English had been spoiled by their victories over the French, and did not try to improve; while the Americans were strict in discipline and were constantly aiming to do better. Our ships, guns, seamanship, and discipline were ahead of those of Europeans at that time. Our people were alert for new ideas, and for the best way of applying them, and the newspapers and patent office reports of that day show how active was the Yankee brain in generating new and wonderful engines of war.

Late in October Commodore Decatur, commanding the frigate *United States*, met the British ship *Macedonian*, which had been captured from the French. The British guns were 18- and 32-pounders. The Americans' were 24- and 42-pounders, and the *United States* had three more guns in broadside, and therefore a much heavier battery. This does not, however, explain the completeness of the victory. The Americans displayed so much skill in the handling of their artillery that on board the *United States* the Americans killed and wounded numbered but thirteen, while on the British vessel there were eight times as many, or one hundred and four. The *Macedonian* became one of the most valuable and useful ships of our navy.

The navy department now ordered a squadron, the *Constitution*, *Essex*, and *Hornet*, to make a cruise in the Pacific Ocean to protect our commerce and whaling fleet from the British cruisers. Then, for the first time, our national vessels were seen in that greatest of oceans, in which now we hold possessions, and where the stars and stripes have been planted to stay. When near Brazil, and four days after Christmas, the *Constitution* met the splendid British frigate, *Java*. Ships, guns, and men were very nearly matched, and the fight lasted over an hour. The *Java* was so badly smashed by the American shot that she could not be kept as a prize, and was sunk. The casualties on our side were thirty-four and on the British one hundred and twenty-four.

Two days after Washington's birthday, Captain

Lawrence, in the brig *Hornet*, near Demerara, in British Guiana, gave battle to the British vessel *Peacock*. In fifteen minutes after the first gun was fired the *Peacock* sunk so quickly that Lawrence's men could not save some of the British sailors, and three of the Americans went down with part of the crew of the *Peacock*. Beside the drowned men, thirty-eight of the British and five of the *Hornet* were killed or wounded in battle. The *Hornet* was hardly scratched. No battle showed so clearly that not superior force and valor, for both crews were alike in numbers and bravery, but these joined with superior science, had won the day.

This series of five naval actions, within as many months, shocked but enlightened the British public. The feeling of contempt for American ships, men, guns, and science changed to respect, and taught British naval men a lesson from which they have never ceased to profit. Instead of "a bunch of pine boards floating a bit of striped bunting," they saw in the American heavy frigate the best-equipped war-ship of modern times.

It must never be forgotten that before 1812 there was no "nation" in the United States, in the same sense that there is now. The states were jealous and comparatively hostile to each other. Although the words "nation" and "national" were used, yet it was hard for a Frenchman or Englishman to see in the voluntary confederation of the thirteen states, or of the sixteen, a true nation. Consequently, most of our diplomacy, yes, even our begging for justice, was met with silent contempt. One set of our own politicians declared that the states were foreign to one another, and only a nation in their relation to other powers, or to Europe; but the Europeans could not see even this. It required the insults of France and Great Britain, and the humiliation of the Embargo and Non-intercourse laws, to fall like the blows of a hammer and weld together the states into "a more perfect union." These events served to create one new national spirit, which burst the shackles of sectionalism and of party spirit and fulfilled the desire of Washington, who wanted a truly American character.

CHAPTER XIII.

OUR FLAG KEPT FLYING ON LAKES AND SEAS.

IT was no wonder that our army failed in this war, for the war department was poorly organized, and few of the officers in the higher grades had seen any service since the Revolution. It was proposed to invade Canada, but there were no roads worth speaking of, over which to march or take wagon-trains; the Indians were unfriendly. On the other hand, the Canadians were skilled watermen, who were likely to do better in the forests and along the lakes and rivers than our men could hope to do.

The British government sent Admiral Sir John Warren to command the British squadron on the American coast. His next in command, Rear-Admiral Cockburn, kept the coast of Chesapeake Bay in alarm by raiding the barnyards and villages of the region, capturing and destroying also Havre de Grace in Maryland and Hampton in Virginia.

One of the ablest men in the British navy was Captain Broke. He was in command of the frigate *Shannon*, which was named after a river in Ireland. This was one of the few vessels of the British navy on which the constant drill of marines and sailors, with cannon and small arms, with the firing of ball cartridges in practice, was steadily kept up. On the first of June, he sent a challenge to Captain James Lawrence, who, after the sinking of the *Peacock*, had been put in command of the frigate *Chesapeake*. Before it arrived Lawrence sailed out of Boston harbor to give battle to this, the finest vessel in the British navy. In the eyes of sailors, the *Chesapeake* was considered unlucky, because in launching, her hull had stuck on the ways and she had reached the water with difficulty, and because also she had been "leopardized" or fired into, without ability to return the attack by the British man-of-war *Leopard*, and had struck her flag. The *Chesapeake* had only a raw crew, hastily gathered, many of them foreigners, and Lawrence had no time to drill them. The crew, equipment, and state of discipline on Lawrence's vessel were entirely different from those on any American ship in the navy. The sailors were a bad lot, disaffected, and clamorous for grog and promises of prize money. They had to be bribed to go to their duty. The forces of the two ships in power of iron and human muscle were about matched, but the *Shannon*, beside having a brave and skilful commander, had an excellent crew in the highest state of efficiency, and it is ever the man more than the machine that tells.

The British captains of this time preferred what they called "yard-arm engagements." By this they meant that after the first broadside their ships should be quickly ranged up alongside of the enemy so that the yard-arms of both could interlock or lie parallel. Then the grappling-irons could be thrown out, boarders could stream over the enemy's side and his ship be taken by assault, final victory being won by hand-to-hand fighting. This allowed sailors to do at sea very much what the British soldiers did on land — they fired a volley and then charged with a cheer, to finish with the bayonet.

Hitherto, however, in the naval duels between American and British ships, the superior seamanship of our captains had prevented such a movement, and the cool scientific gunnery of our men had effectually spoiled the old programme. Now, unfortunately, at the first fire, the *Chesapeake* lost several of her officers, including her commander, Lawrence. He was mortally wounded and carried below, crying, "Don't give up the ship." Then the *Shannon* got into position where she could rake the doomed vessel. This is always the most murderous part of a sea battle, for instead of the ball, canister, and grape-shot tearing across the ship sideways, the missiles fly from stern to stem along the decks, where hundreds of men are crowded together. In this way every shot is apt to do fivefold execution

Very soon after the *Chesapeake* had been raked, losing most of her officers, a boarding party, led by the brave Captain Broke himself, reached the deck of the *Chesapeake*. The cowardly crew without discipline or officers retreated, but the brave chaplain took up the sword and stood his ground, taking off Broke's arm. After a fifteen minutes' fight, the *Chesapeake* was carried as a prize to Halifax. About half a ton of iron, mostly in the form of "langrage" shot from the American carronades, was taken out of the sides of the *Shannon*. This "flying cutlery," made by sewing up old bits of iron and metal scraps of all sorts in bags of leather, was very effective at short range in cutting the enemy's sails and rigging to pieces.

The *Chesapeake*, after being actively used in the British navy for many years, was finally sold and broken up. Her timbers, some of them still marked with the shot of the *Shannon*, were used to build a flour mill. This still stands in use at an English village within a few miles of Portsmouth. Captain Broke was made a nobleman. Provost Wallis, then a young officer on the *Shannon*, lived to be an admiral and died within this decade. Lawrence's last cry, "Don't give up the ship," became a household word in the United States, and was soon the augury of triumph on Lake Erie.

Commodore Isaac Chauncey, on the 9th of November, 1813, obtained control of Lake Ontario. Beside handling his little schooners with ability, he had fresh ships built, and then supported General Pike in an attack upon the Canadian town of York, which was captured, and a ship also. Unfortunately some of our men burned the little parliament house, which afterward gave Admiral Cockburn an excuse for his disgraceful incendiarism at Washington. Fort George, at the mouth of the Niagara River, was also captured by the American flotilla and forces. Two young men who afterward became famous, Captain Oliver Hazard Perry and Lieutenant-Colonel Winfield Scott, took part in this gallant affair. Yet on the whole the campaign on the northern frontier was marked more by failures than by successes. Indeed, the American prospects in the early part or the first half of 1813 were very gloomy, when suddenly a great bright light of victory burst upon the nation.

Oliver Hazard Perry had been sent to Lake Erie to take the naval command. This Ohio region was so very far away in those days from New York and Philadelphia, that a grape-shot cost nearly its weight in silver, and powder was worth as much as spices, but then wood for fuel and shipbuilding was cheap and plentiful. Setting out in a sleigh with his younger brother, he rode through the Mohawk Valley and the woods of western New York. He reached the town of Erie, to which gangs of ship carpenters, who had travelled from Philadelphia by wagon, boat, and canoe, had also come. The shores of the lake furnished all the requisite floating material in the forests which then stood miles deep. The axemen, carpenters, and blacksmiths began their work, and keels were laid and forges set up. Often what was standing timber in the morning would be part of a ship before sunset. So green was the wood of this hastily improvised squadron, that the hammer which struck too far upon the nail head would squeeze out the sap until the hammer's face was wet and the carpenter must look out lest the sap fly in his eyes. When the Kentucky men, who had never seen boats bigger than batteaux, came on board these ships, they were surprised beyond measure at the largeness of the "big canoes."

At the mouth of the bay, beside which the ships were built and launched, there was a bar of sand making shallow water. This was hard to get over any time, and under the fire of the enemy would be impossible. But long ago a Dutchman had invented what is called the "ship's camel," which is a long box or series of caissons of wood joined together. These, when filled with water, sink under a ship, just as a camel kneels to receive its burden. When the water is pumped out of the boxes, they lift the ship up and carry it like a camel under his packs. With these, Perry got over the bar. His squadron consisted of nine vessels, two of which were the brigs *Lawrence* and *Niagara*. On the 14th of September he advanced to meet Commodore Barclay, who was one of Nelson's veterans. The battle took place near Put-in Bay, Ohio. Perry, hoisting over his flag-ship *Lawrence*, on a big square flag, the dying words of the commander after whom the ship was named, "Don't give up the ship," dashed at the enemy. The wind was light. The *Lawrence* was left without much support from his other vessels, and was so exposed to the protracted British fire that her guns were all disabled and nearly all her men killed or wounded. It looked like a complete defeat for the Americans. At this darkest hour Perry, with those of his crew who were less severely wounded, lowered his boat and with his little brother passed through the terrific fire of cannon and musketry to the *Niagara*. Although splashed with water from balls which pierced clothing, splintered oars, and struck all around, the gallant commodore and his men reached the ship and sent Captain Elliott to bring up the schooners in the rear.

It was in attempting to perform a similar feat of rowing between the Dutch and British fleets that an English admiral was killed. Our Commodore

Tattnall, in Chinese waters nearly a half century afterward, though in as great danger as Perry, was similarly successful.

Re-forming his ships in line abreast, and the wind increasing, Perry broke the enemy's line and captured the entire British squadron — the first time such a thing had happened in the history of the navy of Great Britain. Then Perry sat down and dictated that famous sentence of nine words. "We have met the enemy and they are ours." In his nervousness, as seen in the original letter, he left out one word. Brevity is not only the soul of wit, but of fame also, and the glory of a victor is usually enhanced by short sentences that stick in memory.

In nature the soap bubble becomes more gorgeous in color and richer in prismatic tints as it becomes thinner. So the "bubble reputation," which ambitious patriots seek "even at the cannon's mouth," takes on richer rainbow hues when, with the breath of rhetoric, it catches the popular attention. Half of Oliver Perry's fame is due to his sententious despatch of nine words: "We have met the enemy and they are ours." Thomas Jefferson won renown by his pen in the same way. So also did Sheridan and Grant in our day.

The British captured ships were used to transport General Harrison's troops to Malden, while the

Kentucky cavalry marched round the shore of the lake. When the British forces retreated, they were pursued by our horsemen. In the battle on the 5th of October, near the Moravian towns, the united forces of British Canadians and Indians were defeated by Harrison, and Tecumseh was killed. This series of victories gave us peace and quiet on Lake Erie and throughout the Northwest.

In the South four columns of invasion entered Alabama to destroy the Creek Indians, who had listened to the persuasions of Tecumseh, massacred hundreds of whites, and then fortified the Horseshoe Bend of the Tallapoosa River, where they believed themselves safe. On the 27th of March General Andrew Jackson led the regulars and militia to the attack. The volunteers and friendly Indians made the assault in the rear, while the regular army stormed the works in front. For five hours a terrible battle raged, and both parties fought like savages. Even after the firing was over, no prisoners were taken, and the Indians were put to death as if they were vermin. In truth, the Americans were guilty of many frightful excesses and unnecessary cruelties during this war.

CHAPTER XIV.

"OLD IRONSIDES" AND COTTON BALES.

ONE of the most wonderful achievements on the ocean was that of Captain David Porter in the frigate *Essex*. At this time our American whalers were numerous in the Pacific, but were mostly unarmed, while the British whaling-ships carried cannon and were privateers, we thus being at a disadvantage. The situation was relieved by the appearance of the *Essex*. Porter captured thirteen excellent vessels, sending some to the United States, and fitting out others as cruisers.

For a time Porter and his men occupied the Marquesas Islands, which Mendaña the Spaniard had long ago discovered and named. This was either after the wife of the viceroy of Peru, or because the natives seemed to be so polite and well dressed that they were called marquises. The northwestern islands near by, and until late in this century considered a separate group, were discovered in 1791 by an American merchant navigator, named Ingraham, and named the Washington Islands. Tattooing and cannibalism were both very fashionable among the natives. Only for a few months did the stars and stripes wave over the little archipelago. Then the *Essex* returned to Valparaiso. Near this port two British vessels, the frigate *Phœbe* and the sloop *Cherub*, attacked the *Essex*, and after a long battle captured and destroyed this fine man-of-war, named after the county in Massachusetts in which she was built.

On the other hand, Captain Warrington, in the sloop *Peacock*, captured the British brig *Epervier*, off the coast of Florida, in April. Our new sloop of war *Wasp*, named after the captor of the *Frolic*, took and burned the sloop *Reindeer*, sunk the sloop *Avon*, and destroyed several prizes in the British channel. After this destructive cruise, nothing more was ever heard of the *Wasp*.

By this time the royal government sent a large fleet to the Atlantic coast, which blockaded all our ports, and prevented our national vessels from getting to sea; but American privateers had been commissioned, and went cruising over the ocean to capture British ships. These vessels of various size were swift and well manned, and on many the crews were splendidly drilled. They carried from two to ten guns, usually of long range. On most of them the men were armed with pistol and cutlass. They wore leather hats, strengthened with strips of steel on the top for defence against sword strokes, which were held on by straps of bearskin. These came down over the mouth and chin, giving the wearer a ferocious appearance. Altogether, during the war, our privateers captured about fourteen hundred, and our men-of-war about three hundred British vessels. These were wonderful results, showing also the wastefulness and foolishness of war.

Thus far the British government, having Napoleon to attend to and battles to fight against the French, had carried on a defensive policy during war with the United States; but when Napoleon abdicated, bodies of veteran troops were sent over to America who were expected to do great things in marching from Canada to invade American soil. This British army of twelve thousand men took the same route as that of Burgoyne in 1777, and was supported on Lake Champlain by a squadron consisting of the *Confiance*, *Linnet*, *Chubb*, and *Finch*. Our Commodore McDonough had, beside his flagship *Saratoga*, the brig *Eagle*, the schooner *Ticonderoga*, and the sloop *Preble*, while both parties had a flotilla of gunboats. In Plattsburg Bay McDonough waited until the enemy appeared with a fleet of sixteen vessels, mounting ninety-six guns, and carrying one thousand men. Our force consisted of fourteen vessels, carrying eighty-six guns, served by eight hundred and fifty men. Then, on the 11th of September, began a great battle in perfectly smooth water, the guns being fired at point-blank range. Commodore McDonough showed consummate powers of seamanship. After his starboard battery had been silenced, he was able to veer his ship round, having foreseen and provided for this very event. So, getting in position, and sending out from his port battery rapid and accurate broadsides, McDonough, ably seconded by Captain Cassin, won a splendid victory, destroying the fleet and compelling the British army to retreat to Canada.

This battle of Lake Champlain was really fought with more science and skill, and was far more important in results, than was that of Lake Erie, while McDonough, a veteran of the Tripolitan war, was a more accomplished naval officer than was Oliver Perry. Yet where thousands know of the hero of the short and easily quoted despatch and of many pictures, statues, and eulogies, only tens are familiar with the name and work of McDonough, or know that among those most competent to judge — the officers of the navy — "the battle of Plattsburg Bay is justly ranked among the very highest of its claims to glory." Both Perry and McDonough sprang from that nobly endowed Scotch-Irish stock that has so enriched our country and shed lustre upon her fair name.

The navy of the United States was in a much better condition at the end of the war than at the beginning; but as there were no telegraphs in those days to send news quickly, several naval duels, beside the great land battle at New Orleans, were fought after the treaty of peace had been concluded. When Commodore Decatur, on a dark night, tried to get to sea from New York harbor, his ship, the *President*, struck on the bar. She was badly injured while beating on the sand, so that her power of swift sailing was greatly diminished. Chased by the British squadron and fired upon, a battle began with the *Endymion*, which Decatur dismantled, silenced, and compelled to drop out of the action; but the *President* was surrounded and was obliged to surrender, after having lost twenty-four killed and fifty-five wounded. The British, after refitting this finest sailer known, kept the splendid ship for many years. In a certain instance, during the Mexican war, she actually beat some of our men-of-war by her speed.

One of the most brilliant actions in our history was when Commodore Charles Stewart, in the one vessel *Constitution*, captured two ships in one fight, the *Cyane* and the *Levant*. It required the finest seamanship on Stewart's part to manœuvre and fight one ship with *Old Ironsides*, and at the same time to prevent the other from getting in a position to rake him. This battle was fought on the night of February 20, 1815, and lasted forty minutes.

The *Cyane* had thirty-four guns and the *Levant* thirty-one guns, but the *Cyane* was recaptured by a British squadron. Stewart was born in Philadelphia July 28, 1778, and went to sea at the age of thirteen, becoming captain of an Indiaman before he was twenty. He was also in the French naval war of 1800 and in the Tripolitan campaign. He lived until the year 1869. Well do I remember him.

Captain James Biddle, another officer born in Philadelphia, served in the Tripolitan war, during which he was a prisoner nineteen months. On the 23d of March, 1815, in command of the *Hornet*, he fought one of the finest naval battles of the war, capturing the brig *Penguin*. To close the naval record, Captain Warrington, in the *Peacock*, captured the East India Company's armed sloop *Nautilus*, in June; but on hearing that peace had been declared, released this prize and came home, finding all our men-of-war safe in port.

Woman's part in war in nerving heroes to duty, in providing comforts, and in healing and nursing, has been largely overlooked, but the modern historian attends more generously to the facts and truth in this matter. Yet the glory of the mother of heroes and her part in educating them was finely shown, albeit in a homely way, by two Rhode Island farmers, as they met on the day after the news from Lake Erie, in 1813. Said one to the other: —

"Well, I see that Mrs. Perry has licked the British."

"What? It was Oliver, her son, who did it; you mean him?"

"No, I don't; I mean his mother, Mrs. Perry."

"Why?"

"Because she always trained every one of her five boys to keep out of a fight, unless he could not possibly help it; but if he got beaten, she always gave him another whipping when he got home. So Oliver had to win. She made him do it."

On land some of the military operations of the War of 1812 were a disgrace to the country. In the North, General Hull surrendered his forces at Detroit. In the South, General Jackson beat the Creek Indians at Horseshoe Bend on the Alabama River, and completely destroyed their power. Generals Scott, Brown, and Ripley crossed over into Canada, gaining the battle of Chippewa on July 5th, and losing that of Lundy's Lane, though this is often put down falsely as an American victory. On the Potomac there was something like a battle fought at Bladensburg, in which the American militia ran away. Admiral Cockburn, who disgraced the British name, marched into Washington and set fire to the capitol, the executive mansion, and other public buildings, in revenge for the Americans having burnt government edifices at York, the capital of Canada.

Then moving on to Baltimore the British fleet and army tried to take Fort McHenry, but after a twenty-four hours' bombardment were unable to do so. Our country gained by this British defeat the stirring song of "The Star-Spangled Banner." Francis Scott Key, an American who was prisoner on board a man-of-war, wrote the stanzas as in the morning he saw that "our flag was still there."

The one brilliant victory on land was the battle of New Orleans, which was fought fifteen days after a treaty of peace had already been signed, for there were no telegraphs in those days. Great Britain had been occupied in Europe during most of this our second war for independence, and could not send a large army to our country until after the battle of Leipsic. Then fifteen thousand British veterans under the command of General Pakenham, who had been Wellington's quartermaster, were despatched to the mouth of the Mississippi to take New Orleans, and thus control the navigation of the great river.

General Andrew Jackson was put in command of the American army gathered to oppose the skilled warriors of Europe. Most of his forces consisted of raw, undisciplined militia from Kentucky and Tennessee; but they were skilled marksmen and knew how to handle the rifle. To fortify the city Jackson used cotton bales, which had the great advantage

THE BATTLE OF NEW ORLEANS.

of being tough, and could be easily rolled forward or backward. Commodore Patterson, with his little naval force, greatly hampered the advance of the British fleet, and one fort at Chalmette was so handsomely served that the invaders were kept back nine days. In fact, it was the artillery that really decided the victory, though the slaughter of British infantry at the hands of the riflemen behind the cotton was very great. After General Pakenham and other high officers had been killed, the British gave up the campaign and were soon repatriated, or called home. The victor's statue stands proudly to-day in the centre of Jackson Square, in the city of New Orleans.

On its foreign side the War of 1812 was really our second war for freedom. It gave the world assurance that in all our foreign relations we were not thirteen or eighteen states, but one country. On its domestic side it consolidated the Union. It fulfilled the preamble of the Constitution. Henceforward, there was no more talk about a voluntary confederation, but of a nation. Our naval victories and the battle of New Orleans compelled recognition of our country, not only abroad, but even at home, where the local and sectional had predominated over the national spirit.

In August, 1814, three American and five British commissioners met at Ghent, to arrange a treaty of peace. Yet even while the negotiations were going on, the British veterans were being shipped to New Orleans, and the war party and war newspapers in Great Britain were crying out to have President Madison exiled to some island, even as Napoleon was to be sent to "a lone, barren isle." The *London Times* said of the United States, " Better is it that we should grapple with the young lion when he is first fresh with the taste of our flock, than wait until in the maturity of his strength he bears away at once both sheep and shepherd."

After seven months wrangling and negotiation at Ghent, the treaty was signed December 24, 1814. It was ratified by the Senate February 17, 1815. Yet it did not touch one of the points on which the United States had declared war. Our frigates had sufficiently settled these matters, and our rights on the ocean were respected. No foreign nation was likely ever to establish itself on our territory. Through the development of our own industries in mills and founderies, we were now able to weave our own cloth from our own cotton and wool, to make our own tools and machines, no longer depending upon Europe.

Unique and wonderful was the record of the frigate *Constitution* in the two wars, Tripolitan and British. Within three years she had been twice chased by squadrons, fought three big battles, and captured five large men-of-war. She never lost a mast or went ashore, and but few of her crew or officers had been killed or wounded; but then, she was always well manned and commanded. Men are more than ships or guns.

Years afterward, when it was proposed to break up this historic leader of the naval triumphs of 1812, Dr. Oliver Wendell Holmes wrote the poem "Aye, Tear her Tattered Ensign Down," and popular feeling demanded that she be repaired and kept afloat. This was done. Safely housed and roofed over, the *Constitution* has held a conspicuous place of honor on several great naval celebrations, one as late as the Peace Jubilee of 1898, and on the occasion of her own centennial. Visited by tens of thousands of people, her roominess, her great breadth, and the facilities for comfort of officers and men have surprised those familiar with the narrow vessels of to-day.

It is a curious fact that both our first and "our second war for freedom" were fought while King George III, the monarchical figure-head of Great Britain, was living. Born in 1738, he suffered long from insanity, and died in 1820. Our flags, then containing twenty-three stars, hung at half mast in sympathy with a narrow and weak-minded, a well-meaning but unfortunate man.

CHAPTER XV.

MADISON AND MONROE.

IMMEDIATELY after the peace of Ghent, Decatur sailed with a powerful squadron of eleven ships, including some captured from the British, to settle with the Dey of Algiers, who had begun seizing our ships. Great was the surprise of the Barbary ruler, who supposed the naval power of the United States to have been entirely wiped off the seas by the British. Instead of this, a big Yankee squadron appeared, in which were several vessels taken in battle from the very power that had been expected to destroy the American navy. Decatur's ships were the *Guerrière*, *Macedonian*, *Epervier*, *Constellation*, *Ontario*, *Firefly*, *Shark*, *Flambeau*, *Torch*, and *Spitfire*. Two Algerine corsairs were at once captured.

The American eagle bears in his talons the arrows of war and peace. The Divan was given choice of either, for Decatur had on hand a new treaty, already declaring that tribute was abolished forever. The Dey wanted time to consider. He even pleaded for three hours. The reply to his envoy was:—

"Not a minute. If your squadron appears in sight before the treaty is actually signed by the Dey and sent off with the American prisoners, ours will capture it."

Pretty soon an Algerine ship did come in sight, and our men cleared for action; but, although the messenger with the treaty had to row five miles to the shore and back, the Dey signed inside three hours. Within forty-one days after the squadron had left American waters, the American Consul-General landed with honor, and all claims were paid and captives restored. Decatur chivalrously restored two Algerine vessels which we had captured.

One day the minister of the Dey remarked sorrowfully to the British Consul as follows: "You told us that the Americans would be swept from the sea in six months by your navy, and now they make war upon us with some of your own vessels which they have taken."

Thus had our naval officers, Preble, Bainbridge, Decatur, and their gallant subordinates, in the classic waters of the Mediterranean, by a series of brave actions, laid the foundations of our navy's noble reputation. They blew to atoms both the gunboat policy and the claims of robber rulers to molest our commerce and enslave our citizens, and they won the freedom of the seas and the rights of the sailor in the War of 1812. The Pope of Rome paid a high tribute of praise to our little country, declaring that the United States had done more to humble the pride of the Mohammedan pirates than all Europe.

Our navy, originally created in the interests of civilization, has been throughout all its history an instrument to the humbling of the tyrants' pride and the advance of freedom throughout the world. The stars and stripes have become "the symbol of light and law" and the hope of the nations. Columbia is "the gem of the ocean."

> "Thy mandates make heroes assemble
>   When liberty's form comes in view;
> Thy banners make tyranny tremble
>   When borne by the red, white, and blue."

Later on Commodore Bainbridge arrived in the Mediterranean, with the line-of-battle ship *Independence* carrying seventy-four guns. This was the first war vessel of that type which floated our flag in this favorite cruising ground of our officers. A number of these big ships were built in our shipyards. They carried from seventy to one hundred guns, and were named after states and statesmen. They were the *Independence, Washington, Franklin, Columbus, North Carolina, Ohio,* and *Vermont,* while the *Pennsylvania* was pierced for one hundred and twenty guns. Nevertheless, very little value or satisfaction was ever derived from the wooden line-of-battle ships. Such a ship was an Old World idea, which would not work well with Americans. Most of their old hulks have become receiving ships at navy-yards. The frigates were always useful.

Our excellent example was soon followed by the British and Dutch. Under Lord Exmouth and Admiral Van der Capellen, Algiers was bombarded and burned. The next day the Dey signed the treaty, by which he agreed to treat prisoners of war according to Christian customs. He then released 1642 Christian slaves, or counting in those from Tunis and Tripoli 3000. Great was the joy in many homes throughout Christendom. Yet barbarism is easier to coerce than to cure.

When the next Dey came in power, he kidnapped the daughters of European residents for his harem, and sent plague ships about the Mediterranean to spread pestilence, thus making himself an international nuisance.

It is hard for a thief to thoroughly reform. The Dey of Algiers denounced the treaty of 1815, dismissed our Consul, and then wrote our President a letter, in language such as a polite cutthroat might pen, as follows: —

"His Majesty the Emperor of America, its adjacent and dependent provinces, coast, and wherever his government may extend; our noble friend, the support of the kingdoms of the nation of Jesus, the pillar of all Christian sovereigns, the most glorious among the princes, elected amongst many lords and nobles; the happy, the great, the amiable James Madison, emperor of America — may his reign be happy and glorious, and his life long and prosperous."

But President Madison, replying the next year, in 1816, said quietly and without any flower gardens of rhetoric: —

"The United States, whilst they wish for war with no nation, will buy peace of none. It is a principle incorporated into the settled policy of America, that as peace is better than war, war is better than tribute."

When, therefore, the American squadron under Commodore Chauncey appeared in 1817, the treaty was immediately renewed. Thus the United States was the first nation to abolish tribute, and to compel the Barbary powers to treat prisoners of war in a Christian manner. The greatest blessing we won, out of these difficulties, was a navy with noble traditions and prestige. Though such a force was expensive, yet our diplomatic negotiations with the Barbary states had cost as much and even more, that is, between three or four million dollars.

English and French ships, in 1819, blockaded the Algerine ports and made the barbarian Dey behave himself. The insult to the French Consul, in 1827, exhausted French patience. After a three years' blockade of the port an army was landed in Algiers, and the country put under military control and kept as a colony of France during forty years, or until 1871, when the country was given a civil administration.

Out of this French occupation emerged into history the Zouaves, or native Algerian troops, serving at the papal court in the French army and under the French flag on both sides of the Mediterranean and in the Crimea. During our own Civil War this picturesque costume was for a while borrowed by some of our volunteer regiments, but soon abandoned as a rather expensive novelty and less suitable than the blue blouse and trousers. Gradually the native Algerians were separated, and became known as the Turcos, while the Zouaves became almost entirely French. After the Commune had been suppressed, and the army entered Paris, the Zouave organization was dissolved.

In 1876 it compelled great contrasts with those early days, when our navy won fame and set an example to the world in the classic waters of the Mediterranean, to have these once Barbary powers coming with us in peaceful rivalry and exhibiting their products at the Centennial Exposition at Philadelphia.

The next President was James Monroe, after whom the "Monroe Doctrine" was named. This meant that the United States, while resolving not to meddle with the affairs of the nations of the Old World, were equally determined that these should not unjustly interfere in the affairs of the New World. Our people believed that the different nations in the two Americas had a right to manage their own business, without interference from Europe. In his message of December 2, 1823, President Monroe said, "We should consider any attempt on their part to extend their system to any portion of this hemisphere as dangerous to our peace and safety," and interference with American politics anywhere, as "the manifestation of an unfriendly disposition toward the United States."

Most of the countries of Central and South America had thrown off the yoke of Spain and declared themselves for self-government. The monarchs of Europe looked with contempt and fear upon all republics or government "of the people, for the people, and by the people." It seemed as though Spain was trying to get the other one-man powers of Europe to compel the Spanish-American republics to revert to despotism, and wear again the yoke of obedience to the old country. The proposition of a union of English-speaking peoples against Spanish encroachment came first as a suggestion from the British statesman, George Canning, but Mr. Monroe adopted the idea with improvement and enlargement.

We may here give one example of how even contemptible little countries like Portugal looked down upon republics. When Lieutenant Matthew Calbraith Perry called upon the Portuguese Governor at Teneriffe, in the Canary Islands, in 1815 or 1816, he offered to tender a salute to the Portuguese Governor, provided the compliment was returned gun for gun. The Governor replied that it would give him great pleasure to reply to the salute, but with one gun less, as it was the custom of Portugal to return an equal number of guns only to acknowledge sovereigns, but to republics one gun short. Perry plainly replied that as the United States acknowledged no nation as entitled to greater respect than itself, no salute would be fired, and so the American man-of-war went out in silence.

Monroe had been a student who left his college in Virginia and books to be a soldier in the Revolutionary War. He was at the battle of Trenton. Now as President he took his oath of office, near the ruins of the burnt capitol in Washington. His colleague, Vice-President Tompkins, had been the great war Governor of New York in the campaigns of 1812–1815. Tompkins first proposed officially the abolition of slavery in the

Empire State, and after him one of its central and most beautiful counties is named.

Under Mr. Monroe "an era of good feeling" began. The President travelled through New England, where many of the old Revolutionary veterans were delighted to see him wearing the old buff and blue. All sections of the country were reunited in fresh loyalty to the government. The nation gratefully remembered its heroes and made generous provisions for the old soldiers, pensioning the veterans of the war and their widows to the extent of $65,000,000.

CHAPTER XVI.

THE SEMINOLE AND BLACK HAWK WARS.

THE next war that broke out, when our regular army consisted of about ten thousand men, became a fresh occasion for the increase of United States territory. Florida was still a Spanish possession, and in the swamps called the Everglades roamed a tribe of Indians called Seminoles. Government by the Spaniards did not amount to very much beyond the two towns of St. Marks and Pensacola, so that between runaway slaves, bad Indians, white desperadoes and pirates, the whole territory was a menace to the people of the South. The President ordered General Andrew Jackson, with the regulars and volunteers from Georgia and Tennessee and some friendly Creek Indians, to enter the region and secure quiet.

Jackson's campaign was vigorously conducted. Two Englishmen charged with inciting the Indians to incursions and massacre were tried by court martial, sentenced to death, and hanged. This act of Jackson excited great indignation in Great Britain and Spain. It also raised perplexing questions of diplomacy, which, however, were settled in 1819, when Spain ceded Florida to the United States for the sum of $5,000,000. Our southern frontier was thus rectified and sixty thousand square miles were added to the United States. On July 10, 1821, the red and yellow flag of Spain was hauled down, and that of the United States, with thirteen stripes and twenty-four stars, was hoisted at all the military stations. During the next year Florida was organized as a territory, but from 1835 to 1842 was the scene of almost constant Indian wars.

The Seminoles had agreed to remove west of the Mississippi, but the ratification of the treaty was delayed in Congress, and meanwhile the red men of the swamps became dissatisfied and refused to go, while outrages were committed by both whites and Indians. The tribe was divided — one-half agreeing to go west, while the other half was violently excited by Osceola, a half-breed. This man of spirit and ability had felt himself injured, because his wife, a fugitive negro slave, had been taken away from him by her owner. When Osceola protested, using language which the army officers considered insulting, he was imprisoned for a time and was ever afterward bitter and revengeful.

Matters began to look very warlike, yet few preparations were made to guard against danger. On the 28th of December, as Major Dade and a detachment of 110 men were moving through the swampy country, and the dark woods hung with long, low beards of Florida moss, unable to see their deadly foes, they were ambuscaded and surrounded by invisible marksmen. After a long and brave fight every white man was killed, except three or four who feigned death and escaped to tell the tale, which is still recalled by the stone pyramid commemorating the sad event. After a good deal of military activity, in which the Seminoles showed surprising ability in war, they first agreed to move west late in 1837, and then refused once more. Osceola was captured by stratagem. In other words, he was decoyed within our lines. Then, by the base treachery of our army officers, he was knocked down, seized, and put in prison, where he died — another foul blot on our country's history. Although Generals Scott, Clinch, Heustis, Jessup, Taylor, and Worth took part in this Seminole war, it was not until 1842, after an enormous loss of life and money, that the Seminoles yielded and crossed the Mississippi. It is more than probable that General Worth, by his truth, honor, wisdom, and kindness to the Indians, accomplished as much as all the bullets and shell of the soldiers.

It costs vastly more to kill a red man than to educate him. Sooner or later the nation has to pay in blood and tears and money for cruelty, treachery, and unrequited toil, whether of red, black, or yellow humanity. Occasionally it is good to review a war, after the blood and glory are over, and to sum up results. How was it in the matter of the whites and Seminoles? Osceola was the son of an Englishman, named William Powell, and an Indian mother. When but twelve years of age he had come under the influence of Tecumseh. He cared nothing for money gained by robbery, and would allow no scalping or mutilation of the dead. He never forgot a kindness. His wife was the daughter of a fugitive slave, and was stolen from him because she was a slave, and when Osceola demanded her release, using rough language, Colonel Thompson ordered him put in irons.

The awful results of this lack of tact in dealing with a proud-spirited Indian were seen. Within six months Thompson was murdered, a battle took place, Dade's men were massacred, the forts attacked, and in the spirited actions which followed the Indians more than held their own against great odds. Finally it was only through the white man's treachery that Osceola was seized. It was like caging an eagle to put this chief in prison, and his proud spirit wore out his body. His death at Fort Moultrie, January 20, 1838, was worthy of a noble son of the forest. Calling for his best war dress, he put it on. Then, unable to speak, but bidding by grasp of the hand his warriors and captors farewell, he drew out his war knife from its sheath, held it in his right hand, and crossing the blade over his left on his breast breathed his last.

Thus ended one of the most disgraceful chapters in the history of a long "century of dishonor" in which Americans have been both cruel and treacherous to the sons of the soil. The whole story of the Florida war illustrates again the wastefulness and the wickedness of much of our dealing with the Indians.

What is called Black Hawk's War, in which Abraham Lincoln took part as a captain of volunteers, broke out in 1832. As chief of the Sac Indians, Black Hawk had resisted the settling of Illinois by the white immigrants from the East, and in the War of 1812 had taken the part of the British. Later, he and the Sacs and Foxes had been removed from their old hunting-ground on the east side of the Mississippi River and compelled to go westward. At sixty-five years of age, still restless, dissatisfied, and ambitious, he recrossed the Mississippi River, hoping to recover the lands formerly held by his tribesmen. All such hopes, whether of Pontiac, Tecumseh, or Black Hawk, are in vain. He and his warriors were defeated, first by Colonel Dodge, and then, finally and completely, at Bad Axe, Michigan, in August, 1832, by General Henry Atkinson. Again the tribe was removed westward. Black Hawk, his sons, and a few warriors were kept for a while as hostages. They were brought to the eastern cities that they might see the power of the white men and learn how foolish resistance was.

I have heard from my father, who knew Black Hawk, of the personal dignity of this chief. Nevertheless the inland Indians do not like the salt sea or the sea air. On one occasion the sachem and his braves were in charge of my father, while going from one city to another on the Atlantic coast. They squatted in their blankets, smoking their calumets, in a cosey, sheltered corner below deck, when some sailor happened to open a hatchway that let in a blast of cold air and spray. Instantly the whole party rose up and fled to the cabin, grunting out, "Ugh! ugh!"

Under President Monroe the great national road was built from Wheeling through to the Mississippi, and soon the traffic was immense, as the great march toward the setting sun continued.

In 1824-1825 La Fayette visited the United States, and everywhere received a warm and gratifying welcome. To this day, the large number of cities which have in them a La Fayette Street or Avenue, and of towns and counties named after him, show

how deep was the impression he made upon our grandfathers. In Philadelphia, when a salute was fired in his honor from old cannon used in the Revolution, he recognized one, that had its muzzle worn on the under side, as the piece which he himself had saved during his skilful retreat from Barren Hill to Valley Forge, even after a British cannon shot had dismounted it. Lashing the gun to a wagon belonging to John Harby, my own great-grandfather, though its muzzle dragged over the rough and stony road, La Fayette saved the piece. He drew off his men, also, whom the British and Hessians had hoped to surprise and make prisoners. I used to hear, from my grand-aunts and grandmother, who, as children near Valley Forge, had been robbed by the Hessians, the story of La Fayette's impressment of their father's wagon; and how, in 1825, they saw the once young general, now an old man, ride down Chestnut Street in Philadelphia.

The building of other highways to the west continued, but the greatest public improvement, made up to that date in the United States, was in 1825, by which the fresh water of the Great Lakes was poured into the brine of the Atlantic. The Erie Canal was dug to connect the Hudson River at Troy with Lake Erie, a distance of 363 miles, the difference in level being over six hundred feet in favor of Buffalo. As the Dutch had long before conquered up-hill difficulties by the water ladder called a lock, so the state founded by Dutchmen could dig the greatest canal then known. During eight years a great army of laborers cut down the forests, dug the ditch, blasted the rocks, built bridges across rivers, and set the masses of masonry so that the water and boats could be carried upward and over all obstacles.

In 1825, when the work was done, Clinton carried a kegful of the water of Lake Erie and poured it into the Hudson River, in front of New York City, where it is but an arm of the ocean. When the water was let into the artificial river, a line of cannon, five miles apart, boomed the news from one end of the state to the other. The canal was soon paid for by its own revenue. Freight, which used to take three weeks of hauling by wagon and team over roads between Albany and Buffalo, went through in seven days and at one-thirtieth the cost. The whole region west and southwest of New York now attracted an enormous number of settlers from the further east. To-day there is nowhere in the world a finer continuous line of cities than between Boston and Buffalo. Besides the traffic of stage-coaches on land, packet boats bore on the bosom of the canal many thousand passengers to and fro.

Travel soon began to be even more rapid, easy, and inviting, through the invention of the locomotive. Charles Carroll, of Carrollton, who had signed his name to the Declaration of Independence, and who, at ninety years of age, was the lone survivor of fifty-six eminent men, dug the first spadeful of earth for what is now the Baltimore and Ohio railway system. Peter Cooper built the first American locomotive at Baltimore, running it on the road built from Baltimore to Ellicott's Mills. The iron horse excelled so handsomely the one of flesh and blood, both in speed and endurance, that the days of the stage-coach were numbered. The first passenger railway between the Mohawk and the Hudson, or Schenectady and Albany, which began work in 1831, was drawn by the engine John Bull, which was exhibited as a curiosity at the Chicago World's Fair in 1893. John Bull's tender carried several barrels of wood as fuel, and the cars were old stage-coaches set on flanged iron wheels, which ran on strap-iron tracks. As a rule, the railway systems of the United States, especially those first made, ran for the most part from east to west, or in the way that emigration was moving, but at right angles or crosswise to the courses of rivers.

Slavery from the very first had been a dangerous element in our free country, but when the cotton gin was invented, servile labor was made so valuable that negro bondage became more and more a dividing and weakening force in the country. It caused the northern and the southern people first to dislike and then to hate each other. For, while one justified slavery, even going so far as to twist and contort the Bible to support the iniquity, the other not only branded it as "the sum of all villanies," but even denounced the Constitution of the United States for approving of the "institution." Furthermore, the southern people, by raising tobacco, rice, indigo, and cotton, devoting their energies to agricultural production, cared little or nothing for manufacturing enterprises. They wanted to buy their goods and tools in Europe at low rates. The northern people, being manufacturers, had different interests, and wished to prevent European goods from coming in, except under heavy tariff duties. They demanded protection, in order to encourage home manufactures so that they might get rich.

A new era began when Andrew Jackson of Tennessee became President of the United States. He was not only a soldier and immensely popular, being usually called "Old Hickory," but he had new ideas, some of them very bad and some of them very good, about governing the country. Instead of thinking himself, as he ought to have done, the head servant of a country in which the people are the rulers, he administered the government as if it were his family estate. He was without fear, perfectly honest, but very headstrong, and not able always to control his temper. Secretary Marcy, in 1832, had said, " To the victors belong the spoil." Jackson began the shameful "spoils system," removing good servants of the government from office, in order to put in his own partisans. Whereas not more than one or two hundred persons had been by the previous six presidents compelled to resign, Jackson turned out about two thousand. Thus began what was for many years our disgraceful civil service.

Many people were afraid of Jackson because, instead of having had an education in books, or being a dignified Virginian, he was a "western" man; and yet he soon showed that he had some grand ideas about the dignity of the United States government.

When South Carolina, after vainly protesting against the high tariff demanding free trade, declared that after a certain date the laws of the United States would be null and void, and that no duties on goods imported from Europe would be paid, and threatened secession, President Jackson ordered General Scott to Charleston to enforce the laws. This was done, and instead of the "nullification" of the general government, it was the state legislature's resolution that came to nothing.

Already in the Senate of the United States the battle, afterward fought in blood, had begun in words. Robert Hayne and John C. Calhoun feared that the tendency of the East and North was to centralize, and make the national government too strong at the expense of the states. These men upheld the extreme doctrines of state right, state sovereignty, nullification, and secession. On the other side Daniel Webster defended the Union and national supremacy in a series of remarkable speeches. These, widely read, thrilled the American heart all over the land. They educated thousands of young men to be the patriots of 1861. The general effect of this great debate was to consolidate both the South and the North in their differing sentiments. Thus on a grander scale were debated the same great doctrines of national supremacy and state right, the same problems which had been presented to the Federal Dutch republic in the days of Maurice and Barneveldt. Jackson's prompt action maintained the Union. Under Henry Clay's initiation a new tariff was adopted, which for a time satisfied and removed irritation.

So prosperous was the country that, without any public debt, the surplus from the treasury was divided among the different states. The country

was growing rapidly. Pennsylvania coal, the best
in the world, fed the steamboats that were now running
in most of our large rivers, and the "black diamonds"
were everywhere in demand. New canals
were being opened, and railways were constructed,
most of them headed toward the Mississippi. The
great express business was in its infancy. The
foundations of Chicago had already been laid by
the building of a few log cabins. There are still
living men who can remember when this second
city of the United States was but a collection of
rude frame houses.

CHAPTER XVII.

OUR NORTHWESTERN EMPIRE.

JACKSON'S administration was especially noted for the vigor of our foreign policy. France had long owed us large sums from a long series of spoliations at the end of the last and the beginning of the present century. Naples was backward and insolent in refusing to settle just American claims for vessels seized during the reign of Joseph Bonaparte and Murat. By able negotiations France was brought to pay up her debts, but Naples still refused to settle.

Summoning Commodore Patterson, his old comrade in the battle of New Orleans, Jackson ordered him to the Mediterranean. It was so arranged that six of our men-of-war should arrive, one after the other, in the Bay of Naples. This they did in handsome style, ranging their guns opposite the main streets of the city. The result was that instead of the refusal at the beginning of the week, all claims were paid up before the following Sunday.

To extend our trade in the far East, Mr. Edmund Roberts of Portsmouth, New Hampshire, was sent out on the man-of-war *Peacock*. He succeeded in making a treaty with the Sultan of Muscat and with the two kings of Siam. This opened American trade with Zanzibar and the Malay Peninsula. Roberts also opened negotiations with Cochin-China, but was repulsed. He had intended also to go to Peking, and hoped to open trade with Japan, but died prematurely at Macao. Our foreign commerce increased greatly under Jackson's administration.

American enterprise at the ends of the earth was signally illustrated in the Wilkes exploring expedition, from 1838 to 1842, which greatly enriched science. Most of the vast ice-hedged Antarctic continent was discovered and the Samoan and Fiji groups of islands carefully examined. Besides Graham, Alexandra, Wilkes, and Enderby lands, discovered by Commodore Wilkes, the American flag has floated over the Barber, Palmyra, Prospect, Fanning, Christmas, Starbuck, Penrhyn, Swan, Pitt, McKean, and Hull islands in Polynesia. In later years the voyages of Kane and other American explorers have made known the northwestern part of Greenland as far as discovered, called Lincoln and Grant land and Grinnel land on the opposite shore of Smith Sound. Not until recent times has our government made any serious attempt to make known the ownership of islands that are ours by right of discovery.

Although we had no national debt, yet, because of so much speculation and unwise schemes, there broke out in 1837 a financial panic. Not long after that the Mormon movement began, which transformed Utah desert into a garden, and attracted many thousand emigrants from Great Britain, Norway, and Sweden. Steamship lines were established on the ocean, and millions of people crossed from the old fatherlands to the country whose wealth and power not even panic could paralyze.

When in 1845-1846 the potato crop failed in the Emerald Isle, the Irish began to come over to our country by the hundreds of thousands. This led to new developments. Within a few years some of our eastern cities were practically controlled by Irishmen, for Patrick takes naturally to politics and has shown considerable ability in this line of achievement. Besides producing men eminent in every department of life, Ireland gave us many recruits for the regular army and militia, producing a noble type — the Irish-American soldier. The dark side of the Irish is seen in the great amount of drunkenness and liquor selling among them, and is especially shown in lawlessness and wild schemes, such as the so-called Fenian republic, which, after getting many thousands of dollars from servant girls and ignorant people, ended in 1866 and 1867 in an absurd failure in an attempt to attack Canada from the Vermont frontier. Even as early as Van Buren's administration attempts were made to invade Canada, but the would-be invaders were scattered by Colonel McNab of the Canadian militia. One of the few American flags captured by the British and to be seen in a museum at London was taken about this time.

After the United Kingdom, Germany has sent us the largest number of immigrants, followed in their order by Scandinavia, Austria-Hungary, Italy, and Russia. From 1820 to 1893 over five million German-speaking people entered the United States, forming excellent material for the building up of the national commonwealth, because soon absorbed and assimilated. All attempts to keep up foreign languages and peculiar Old World customs and notions in the United States end sooner or later in failure. Common sense wins the day. Gaelic, Dutch, German, and French folks, even the old ones, find that God can be worshipped, friendships maintained, and business done just as well in English as in the language of their ancestors.

In the early forties, when the Dutch King William arbitrarily interfered with the affairs of the Reformed Church in the Netherlands, a large immigration under Dominies Van Raalte and Scholten set toward North America. The immigrants passed through the Mohawk Valley or up the Mississippi

River to Michigan, Wisconsin, Iowa, and Nebraska, where dwell their descendants, now numbering over a hundred thousand, who are among the best people of the United States.

Martin Van Buren was of pure Dutch descent, and one of the ablest of our statesmen. Under him the opposition to slavery was established in politics and a system of nominating presidential candidates in popular conventions carried out. The "free soilers" declared that Congress had no more power to make a slave than to make a king. The words of one political campaign song ran, "Van, Van, is a used-up man." Another one declared for "Tippecanoe and Tyler too." Indeed, from Jackson's time, the American people seem to have had a characteristic weakness for military officers as presidents. The first presidents, both Federalists and Republican-Democrats, had been mainly civilians. The Democrats, after forty years of victory, had to yield now to the Whigs, whose standard-bearer was William Henry Harrison. He was called "the Log Cabin candidate," because after his military campaigns in the Northwest he lived on a farm, on a piece of land cleared of forest trees, on the banks of the Ohio.

I well remember how in my boyhood the mantel-pieces were ornamented with small models, in stone or glazed earthenware, of a log cabin with a coon on the roof and a barrel of hard cider standing by the door. Even in the great political processions, many miles long, there were log cabins on wheels and a live coon on the ridge pole of each. Thus began the great presidential campaigns, inaugurated by the policy of Van Buren, with nominating conventions which blossomed out into enormous parades with torchlights, "wide-awake" uniforms, bands of music, transparencies, banners, and many things funny as well as showy and expensive.

President Harrison died within a month of his inauguration. Then our country had its first, and generally disagreeable, experience of vice-presidents becoming presidents, and John Tyler occupied the chair. During his administration Rhode Island gave up its antiquated government by charter and the old Dutch system of representation by towns instead of by voters. An agreement was made between Great Britain and the United States, called the Webster-Ashburton treaty, by which war was averted, the Maine boundary fixed, and an American squadron under Commodore Perry despatched to Africa, where already Monrovia had been located and settled by freed slaves from America, and Liberia had been erected into a republic.

The next great invention, that of the telegraph, was to give the railroads an amazing development, lay nerves of iron, and send pulses of light under the ocean, and, indeed, give the world a new nervous system, annihilating space and time. Americans from the first were interested in and developed the science which has received its name from the Greek "electron," or amber, because this substance when rubbed attracts and holds hairs or bits of paper and generates "electric" force. Franklin, in Philadelphia, drew sparks from the clouds and invented the lightning rod. Professor Moses Farmer, of Eliot, Maine, was, after Benjamin Franklin, the great American electrician. Most of his experiments and machines anticipated what has since been accomplished in electric traction, lighting, submarine explosion, and telegraphing,—for all these things he accomplished before 1850. Professor Joseph Henry, in the Albany Academy, had discovered that one could ring a bell at a distance, and get other work done by transmission of electric energies through a wire.

Professor S. F. B. Morse, an artist, who, however, did nothing electrical, put Henry's discovery to a grand use. He invented what is called the Morse Alphabet of lines and dots, which made by a telegraphic transmitter could be read as letters, and so made into syllables, words, and sentences. Morse secured from Congress an appropriation of $30,000 to have wires strung from Baltimore to Washington. In the Supreme Court room, in the capitol, he sent and received the message from Numbers xxiii. 23, "What hath God wrought?" Ezra Cornell, of Ithaca, New York, was one of the first to see the vast benefits and commercial value of the new invention. As the Irish servant girl said, "He invented telegraph poles." Instead of stretching wires, two of them in the ground, he conceived the idea of stringing the iron threads, well insulated, up in the air and of using the earth as the return circuit.

Almost as wonderful as this "far-distance writing" were the other American inventions, which one after the other astonished the world, such as the grain elevator and steam shovel, the steam river dredge, wire-card and wire-weaving machine, the eccentric lathe, the revolver, the reaper and mower, the sewing machine, the ship's propeller, the steam printing-press, the type-writer, electric dynamos and motors, the telephone, phonograph, and hundreds of others.

Our territory was again increased, in the spring of 1845, by the annexation of Texas. Sam Houston, Stephen Austin, and many other Americans had settled in the country, then a part of Mexico. Tired of Mexican anarchy they had risen in arms, fought battles with Santa Anna, won a great victory at San Jacinto, and formed an independent republic. After more than one request for admission into the

Union, Texas was annexed by a joint resolution of Congress. Thus a territory five times the size of England was added to the domain of the United States.

James K. Polk's administration was marked by another tremendous expansion of the United States, both on the north and the south of the Pacific coast. Heretofore the great region of the Northwest, between the Rocky Mountains and the Pacific Ocean, and between that part of the North American continent claimed by Russia, and that part below claimed first by Spain and later by Mexico, was an unknown region not definitely belonging to any nation. Captain Gray, in the ship *Columbia*, who first carried the American flag around the world, had named the Columbia River. Van Couver, a British sea captain of Dutch name, had made exploration of the waters around the island which bears his name. Young William Cullen Bryant, a boy just out of college, had written the poem "Thanatopsis," which for a generation or two afterward was a favorite on the school rostrum and elocution platform. In it occurs the words suggesting distance, desolate silence, loneliness, and the unknown dead: —

> "Take the wings
> Of morning ; traverse Barca's desert sands,
> Or lose thyself in the continuous woods
> Where rolls the Oregon, and hears no sound
> Save its own dashing — yet, the dead are there."

It was known that there were splendid mountains, rivers, and fertile lands on that Pacific slope. Yet, though the Spaniards from Ferrelo in 1543, and the Englishmen, Sir Francis Drake in 1578 and Captain Cook, and numerous American explorers and traders had visited the ocean's rim and the beach, none had gone inland to explore. Even the coast-line was but slightly known, until Captain Robert Gray, a Boston trader, entered the mouth of the Columbia River on the 11th of May, 1792, and thus secured the foundation of the American title to Oregon. A trading post was begun in May, 1810, but abandoned in a few weeks. The Pacific Fur Company founded Astoria on March 22, 1811. In 1818 the United States and Great Britain made a treaty of joint occupation. The Hudson Bay Company was at first anxious to have the place kept unsettled, so that wild animals should be numerous and the crop of furs large; but American Christian people, obedient to their Master's command, sent out missionaries as early as 1834. The Methodists founded a mission under Jason Lee, while the American Board sent out Rev. Dr. Parker, who was supported in part by the Presbyterian Church and by the town of Ithaca, New York. It was he who prevailed upon young Marcus Whitman and his wife to come out and help. The bride and groom, though warned that no passage on wheels could be made into Oregon, succeeded in crossing the mountains.

Gradually other Americans came into the country. This roused the fears and jealousy of the British, who wished to claim this region wholly for Great Britain. At a dinner table where Marcus Whitman was present, they expressed their intention of occupying and taking formal possession of the Pacific slope, the following spring. Thereupon Whitman determined to ride to Washington over the mountains, and prairies, and rivers, in the heart of winter and to state the case to President Tyler and ask that the country might be occupied by American settlers. Dressed in frontier costume, he rode through the blizzards, forded or ferried the icy rivers, faced the storms, slipped past the hostile Indians, and, though often near the border line of death from cold and starvation, he reached in health, though terribly frost-bitten and nearly exhausted, the first place he could call home. This was on the doorsteps of Dr. Parker, in Ithaca, where still stands the house at which this heroic missionary, frontiersman, and commonwealth builder arrived.

From Ithaca Dr. Whitman went quickly to Washington, and in the presence of President Tyler and his cabinet argued that the fair and fertile country of Oregon ought to be occupied by American settlers. Getting the government's encouragement, he attracted two hundred families, numbering seven hundred people, to the task of colonization and expansion. With their long wagon trains they moved over the prairies, rivers, and mountains, during the summer of 1843. Settling in the valley of the Oregon, a provisional government was formed and the whole northwestern coast came under the American flag.

There was a good deal of diplomacy necessary before our exact northern boundaries were settled and our frontier rectified. Russia made claims which neither Great Britain nor the United States would allow, and the boundary line northward of the United States, from the Lake of the Woods, had not been settled by the peace of 1783. Yet, although there were great cries of "The British must go," and "Fifty-four forty, or fight," yet the two English-speaking peoples, by the Webster-Ashburton treaty of 1846, settled their differences in a friendly way. The two nations agreed to divide the territory, the Americans taking the land between parallels 42 and 49, which included the great Columbia River and valley, and the British from parallel 49 to Alaska. The actual boundary line was run by surveyors along the 49th parallel, and marked by stones and iron pillars placed a mile apart.

Thus, once more, the Americans became expansionists, and increased the national territory by the addition of more territory than Texas contained, — in Idaho, Washington, and Oregon, or two hundred and fifty-five thousand square miles. All this was obtained by good diplomacy, without an ounce of powder or a drop of blood being wasted.

CHAPTER XVIII.

OLD "ROUGH AND READY" IN MEXICO.

A GREAT many wars arise from mere questions of boundaries. Much bloodshed would have been saved in the history of the world if surveying had been properly attended to, and the chain and cross-staff had been brought in as proof of right, instead of ball and powder. The more engineering enters into questions of land, or what the Germans call "agrar-politik," the less likely are bloody quarrels to arise.

William Penn and his heirs set the good example and precedent of having a correct line drawn by the best British men of science, and his heirs paid pounds, shillings, and pence for the good work done. Washington was as good an engineer and surveyor as he was a general and statesman. Wisely did President Cleveland recommend, and Congress appropriate money for, the Venezuela Boundary Commission. Great Britain was one of the first countries to be well measured and mapped, and to maintain an ordnance survey. With us it became quite early the custom to send out from Washington geological surveyors with exploring parties, so as to see what were the resources of the country.

When new states, especially, are formed, it is above all things necessary first to have the boundaries determined with exactness; or, in Lord Beaconsfield's words, to secure a "scientific frontier." Yet when Texas was admitted as a state in 1845, this question was undecided. The Texans fixed their boundary line at the Rio Grande on the west. They also claimed that all the territory, up to the 42d parallel, on the northwest, was theirs. Mexico, on the contrary, drew the boundary at the Nueces River, or a hundred miles eastward. So here was one of those debatable strips of land, lying between a weak and a powerful nation and almost certain to be grasped and held by the stronger of the two. So it happened with the 50-mile "neutral strip" between China and Korea, which, after remaining unoccupied for two centuries, was in 1877 possessed by the Chinese, and the frontier of China pushed many leagues nearer the rising sun. The policy of Li Hung Chang and President Tyler was the same. The President ordered General Zachary Taylor to occupy the land. Old "Rough and Ready," as he was afterward called, built Fort Texas on the east bank of the Rio Grande. The Mexicans ordered him to leave. He refused. Then the Mexican infantry and lancers crossed over on what President Tyler in his message called "American soil."

On May 1 General Taylor marched out with most of his troops toward Point Isabel, where were his supplies, then threatened by General Arista. In his absence an attack was made on Fort Texas, which was gallantly defended by Major Brown of the seventh infantry, after whom the fort was later named. When Taylor heard of the hostilities begun by the Mexicans, he started on May 7 to relieve Major Brown. General Arista, learning of this, drew off his forces, about six thousand strong, and in the tall grass at a place called Palo Alto waited for the Americans. A battle began which lasted five hours; but, although there was a good deal of firing and smoke, the two armies never got close enough to do much execution. In those days of smooth-bore muskets and "ball and buck," — the cartridges being made of paper and having at the end a big round leaden ball with three buck-shots, — men might fire all day without hitting each other, unless they got within a range of a few hundred feet. When the Americans charged, the Mexicans retreated with a loss of one hundred men. It was the splendid field-gun practice of the Americans that decided the battle, and though Major Ringgold was killed, yet "Ringgold's light artillery" at once became famous.

The next day Arista, having taken up his position

behind intrenchments near the ravine of the palm trees, or Resaca de la Palma, which crossed the Matamoras road about three miles north of the town, hoped to annihilate Taylor's force. This time it was the cavalry that won the victory. Captain Charles May, with his famous dragoons, made a gallant charge, sabring the Mexican gunners, capturing the cannon in the batteries, and pursuing the enemy to the river, making the victory complete.

In place of the gay departure, a few days before, of brilliantly uniformed men, sallying out hopefully to expectant victory, cheered by the smiles and plaudits of beautiful women, was the return of a beaten army to Matamoras discouraged and disorganized. On the 18th General Taylor crossed the Rio Grande and occupied the city, but was unable, from lack of supplies, to follow up his success.

President Tyler sent a message to Congress, saying that the Mexicans had spilled blood on our territory; but Abraham Lincoln, who was a member of Congress from Illinois, introduced what were called the "spot resolutions," demanding to know the exact spot where American blood had been shed. War was duly declared. When a call for fifty thousand volunteers was made, most of the states responded with alacrity, and the enthusiastic volunteers were at once put under discipline and

CAPTAIN MAY'S CHARGE AT RESACA DE LA PALMA.

training by officers of the regular army. The country was determined that the miserable failures of 1812 should not again be repeated. At this time our military officers in the upper grades were men of signal ability, having had long experience in rough lands and the Indian campaigns. The Southern States were especially forward, for the people who believed in servile labor expected to win a large amount of new territory, where black slaves should be worked without wages. Some Power, not ourselves, decided otherwise. It turned out that over all the new region there is not to-day a single slave.

While the new army of militia was being formed, the regulars were waiting for reënforcements, supplies and means of transportation were being furnished, the iron ore in the ground was being transformed into ammunition, the hides fresh from the flocks were being tanned out and sewed into accoutrements, and all the supply train of a great army was being got ready; the Mexicans also prepared for defence and gathered new forces.

At the end of summer General Taylor moved forward into Mexico with his able assistants, Worth, Twigg, and Butler; he reached Monterey, which was a strongly fortified city and amply garrisoned under General Ampudia. Taylor began the battle, which lasted three days. There was heavy fighting and the batteries were taken by assault. Ampudia surrendered on the 24th. Taylor made generous terms, allowing the Mexicans to retire with their arms, though he kept possession of the city.

The plan of campaign as at first made was to invade Mexico from the north by land and in three divisions, — the western, eastern, and centre. Such a campaign meant the spreading of our little army over a vast extent of hostile country where transportation would be difficult and the climate uncertain, while no vital blow could be struck at the enemy. Mexico, the land of the cactus, the eagle, and the serpent, was too large for scattered campaigns. Scientific warfare demands that the enemy be pierced in his vitals.

The best strategy in 1846 required that the main army should land at a point on the seacoast nearest the capital and move at once to capture it, the city of Mexico. Geography is half of war. From the time of Cortez to the last invasion of Mexico, under Napoleon III, the invader's ships have always gathered at Vera Cruz, the Rich City of the True Cross. While the right wing of our army moved to California, and Taylor held the centre, Scott led the left wing by the sea to attack the city of Mexico. So the main preparations by the government at Washington — William L. Marcy being Secretary of War and John Y. Mason being Secretary of the

Navy — were devoted to forming and equipping
Scott's army. Two fleets, one of transports, which
should carry the volunteers to Vera Cruz, and the
other of war vessels, which should capture or blockade the Mexican seaports, were fitted out. In the
Pacific Ocean our warships, under Stockton, were
to keep the enemy in alarm. General Taylor had
to yield to Scott most of his best troops in Quitman's and Worth's division. He thus became,
for a time, little more than a drill-master of raw
volunteers.

At this time our flag had twenty-eight stars, for
Texas was the twenty-eighth state admitted into the
Union. Nine of the new states since 1783 had been
first settled by the French, and one by the Spanish.

The Army of the West, though smallest in numbers, performed a work of great labor and with much
hazard, though with very little popular notice or
glory at the time. Most of this force, consisting of
about eighteen hundred men, were volunteers from
Missouri. Under General S. W. Kearny they
moved against New Mexico and California. Across
the desert, where there was danger of dying from
thirst, beside perils from Indians and from endless
toil, a march of two months began. On the 18th of
August, 1846, they reached Santa Fé. While Colonel Price remained in command of New Mexico,
General Kearny with one hundred cavalry soldiers

pressed on toward the Pacific waters. In this brave and hazardous undertaking he lost some of his men on the march and more in a battle at San Pasquel. When left with sixty troopers, expecting to be entirely cut off, he was delighted to find a rescuing party sent to him overland from our fleet. Our sailors, under Commodore Sloat, had taken possession of Monterey, in California, while Commander Montgomery had seized San Francisco. Captain John C. Fremont, an engineer officer in charge of a surveying party, had raised the American flag at several points. The story of this officer is one of the most romantic in American annals.

Fremont was the son of a French immigrant who, though left an orphan at four years of age, made his own way in the world. Commissioned lieutenant of engineers, he became the great "pathfinder." He explored the Northwest, the Rocky Mountain regions, the wonderful scenery of high California, the Sierra Nevada, the San Joaquin and Sacramento valleys, and the Apache country. He thus made known the geography of our great far western regions. In 1845 he was again on his way to the Pacific. Receiving authority from Washington, he conquered all upper California, and surveyed the route for a great road from the Mississippi to San Francisco. He pierced the hitherto unknown country of the terrible Apaches, and defeated them in battle. He reached Sacramento after a hundred days of marching and surveying.

Already our American pioneers had settled on the river. It was rumored that the Mexicans were negotiating with Great Britain for the sale of California, and that the Mexican Governor, General De Castro, was on the march. The settlers took up arms and joined Fremont's camp. Having captured a Mexican post with some cannon and muskets, he routed De Castro and his force on the 5th of July. The settlers declared themselves independent and elected Fremont Governor of the province, and the American forces, naval and military, were joined at Monterey. Other operations on the Pacific coast were the battles at San Gabriel and the Mesa River, January 8 and 9, 1847, in which the Mexicans failed to regain the ground they had lost. Among other detached enterprises was the capture of Mazatlan under Commodore Shubrick.

Our navy made a brilliant record during the Mexican war, both on the Pacific Ocean and in the Gulf waters. Our blockading vessels were stationed at Tampico, Tobasco, Alvarado, and Tuspan, and prevented supplies from reaching the enemy. The "mosquito fleet" of small gunboats was very useful for service in rivers, and several gallant actions were performed in the capture of these seaport towns. At the beginning, the chief officer in command was Commodore Conner.

These were the days of the infancy of steam in war. The *Missouri*, the *Mississippi*, and the *Princeton* were about the only large war steamers in the American navy. So the Gulf squadron was divided. Commodore Conner, a veteran of the War of 1812, took charge of the sailors, and Commodore Matthew C. Perry of the steamers. Having no ships of light draught, Conner had been able to accomplish little, and the splendid opportunities of the first year were lost. So the main squadron lay idly off Sacrificios Island, out of range of Mexican forts. Spy-glasses were pointed daily at the flag-ship for signals to begin action, but they did not come.

Meanwhile, to rouse the drooping spirits of our tars, Perry planned the capture of Tobasco, where Cortez had fought his first battle. Here lay some vessels and boats, which were just the sort needed for the uses of the squadron. In the big steamer *Mississippi*, towing the *Vixen*, *Bonita*, *Reefer*, *Nonita*, *McLane*, and *Forward*, with two hundred marines from the frigates *Raritan* and *Cumberland*, Perry dashed across the sand bar, almost before the Mexicans knew of his arrival, and captured the town. During the next two days, going up the river with the small steamers and boats to Frontera, this place also was seized, but after the treachery of the

Mexicans was bombarded and evacuated. Our squadron returned safely to Vera Cruz. New spirit was infused into the navy, and the name of Perry became a rallying cry. Tampico, 210 miles north of Vera Cruz, was the next place to be attacked. The city had sent a crack battalion and even an artillery company, made up of deserters from our camps, to Santa Anna's army. Indeed, the crafty Mexican hoped that all of General Taylor's Irish soldiers, who were Roman Catholics, would desert because three or four score had done so. In this Santa Anna was mistaken, for the Irishmen stood faithfully to the stars and stripes. Yet hoping both to weaken the Americans and to strengthen his forces with the Tampico garrison, Santa Anna ordered the city evacuated. As the fleet with the two commodores moved up the river, our men witnessed a beautiful sight. It was the star-spangled banner waving in triumph over the city, and hoisted by a woman's hand. The wife of the banished American Consul bravely remained and welcomed her countrymen. Captain Josiah Tattnall, who afterward in China quoted the famous phrase "Blood is thicker than water," was sent eight miles further up the river, and captured the town of Panuco. Then Perry was despatched with "the pride of the navy," the steam frigate *Mississippi*, to New Orleans.

It was considered a great thing, in those days, that this steamer was able to go so swiftly, first to Matamoras for reënforcements, to get troops from General Patterson for a garrison to hold Tampico, and thence to New Orleans to procure intrenching tools, wheel-barrows, a field battery, soldiers, and provisions, and within one week to deliver these in Tampico. Perry's next exploit was to capture the town of Laguna del Carmen, which he did handsomely. He thus supplied plenty of good food for the squadron.

General Taylor's battles were sanguinary, but not decisive. Mexico was too large to be affected by a little bloodshed on the northern border. Named after the tutelary divinity Mexitl, it is shaped like a cornucopia, 1950 miles long and 750 miles wide in its upper portion, and, tapering in the south, contains 756,232 square miles. It is so vast in area that most of the Mexicans hardly knew there was an American army on the soil. Hence the necessity of striking at the vitals of the country and of sealing the seaports.

While Scott was still in the United States, gathering and drilling his army, Perry was sent north to have the *Mississippi* refitted and to collect lightdraught steamers suitable for blockade duty. These steamers were the *Scourge, Scorpion, Vesuvius, Hecla, Electra, Ætna, Stromboli,* and *Decatur*.

What stinging and volcanic names! Indeed, to savage and half-civilized men the first idea of a steamship is that it has a volcano at work inside the hull and used to turn the wheels.

Santa Anna, relying on the strong fortifications at Vera Cruz to keep back the Americans, gathered a great army in the north, expecting to defeat Taylor and then turn against Scott. Hearing of the Mexican's approach with twenty thousand men, Taylor, who had only five thousand men, mostly new volunteers who had never been in battle, fell back to get the advantage of position on the plain of Angostura. This is near the beautiful place called Buena Vista, which means bellevue or fine outlook. The ground was composed of mountain ridges, narrow defiles, and impassable ravines.

Taylor's fresh volunteers were enthusiastic, and had confidence in their commander. When he rode up and down the ranks and called them his "fighting cocks," they were ready to follow or to stand by their leader, come what might. They were dressed in blue roundabout coats, and blue trousers with white stripe along the side, and wore flat round caps. They carried muskets and white cross-straps and belt.

The first battle, which began on Washington's birthday, was little more than a skirmish. The next day Santa Anna hurled his whole force with terrible energy upon the American column, but our men stood firm. Fortune varied. The Mexicans, after being repeatedly beaten back, returned resolutely to the charge. Both sides showed equal bravery and obstinacy. At last Santa Anna, finding that he made no progress, had to give up and retire. The American loss was about seven hundred, and the Mexican twenty-five hundred, beside a large number of deserters. The Americans were in control of the battlefield and of that district of country.

CHAPTER XIX.

THE NAVY AND ARMY AT VERA CRUZ.

THE largest squadron that had heretofore ever assembled under the American flag—steamers, sailing ships, and bomb vessels—was put under command of Commodore M. C. Perry. Yet so economical was our government, that this Matthew, the brother of Oliver, the hero of Lake Erie, though called a commodore, was only a captain with a broad pennant. The scores of transports carrying the volunteers were delayed at the Bahama Islands, waiting for a change of wind, and there were passed by the swift steamers. After many of those vexatious delays, which so try the spirits of young volunteers, they at last caught sight of the crosses over the cathedral and churches in the Rich City of the True Cross, and perching on them the vultures, which in Spanish cities are the black scavenger angels. In 1899, after the Americans had cleared the streets of Santiago in Cuba, the vultures began to starve.

As day by day ships came in with flags flying

and bands of music playing, loaded with enthusiastic volunteers from the North, a floating city gathered in the harbor, or rather the offing, of Vera Cruz. It was necessary to act promptly, however, for during six months of the year the vomito, or yellow fever, threatened the lives of all foreigners. The disease is bred through climatic conditions, but its coming is encouraged and its ravages are aggravated by the filth which gathers in most Spanish towns, where there is usually a lack of proper drainage. The other half year was marked by the northers, or terrific wind-storms from the north, which are very destructive to shipping. In those days, there being no wharves or moles, ships lay at anchor at some distance from the city or fastened to iron rings in the walls.

Preparations were now made for the landing of twelve thousand troops. To do this in the surf, out of range of the guns of the city and the great castle of San Juan d'Ulloa, was no easy task. Usually on such occasions, as for example at the French landing in Algeria, many men were drowned. By the skill of our naval officers and sailors, who used large flat boats made in the United States, all the soldiers, with artillery and supplies, were landed safely.

Intrenchments were dug and cannon and mortar platforms built. The line of circumvallation, when completed, was named Camp Washington. It was impossible for the army to march into the interior, and thus gain the healthy highlands, until the walled city of Vera Cruz had been reduced, and yet General Scott had only a pitiful array of ordnance to batter down the heavy walls built of coquina, or shell rock. Ten mortars and ten 24-pounder guns were indeed soon mounted, but the forty other mortars and the heavy guns were somewhere at sea on transport ships, with no news of them or their whereabouts. Every day the dreaded yellow fever came nearer. Easily propagated by mosquitoes and flies, an outbreak among our troops would mean a ruinous pestilence. The light army cannon could not batter down the walls. To throw shells into the city would only kill women and children without making the enemy surrender. In such a strait, what could General Scott do?

When Perry, on March 20, 1847, arrived back from New York, the Mexican batteries were firing in a lively way on our men and camps, but no response yet came from the American side. That night it blew a gale from the north, hiding the vessels in spray and the camps in sand.

General Winfield Scott was one of the ablest officers that the United States army has ever known. Born in 1786, he entered the service in

1808. He was not only a veteran of the War of 1812, in which he had won glory and a gold medal, but had served in the campaigns against the Indians. It was he who had elaborated the system of tactics which then formed the basis of instruction in the United States army. He was a thoroughly scientific soldier and a very humane man. He considered it disgraceful to spill one drop of blood, or to have one life lost more than was necessary. Instead of "a big butcher's bill," and great lists of killed and wounded, his idea of war was to secure results without waste of human life by disease, battle, or soldier's vices. Furthermore, he was desirous of inflicting no more loss upon the enemy than was absolutely necessary, though in time of need he spared neither his men nor the foe. He planned the campaign in such a way that much money, but little fight, would be required. Yet the Washington authorities had not very liberal ideas and at first set Scott aside. Afterward they were obliged to recall him and put him in authority. His plan was to move immediately from the malarial seacoast up into the mountains, to capture Mexico City and quickly end the war.

Santa Anna, however, calculated that Vera Cruz would hold out a long while. Then he expected that two of his allies, Commodore Norther would wreck the fleet, while General Vomito would ruin the army. So, also, the Spaniards calculated in 1898.

Now at Vera Cruz, having opened his batteries and found his guns too light, Scott was bitterly disappointed. With all his greatness, he was an exceedingly vain man. Magnificent in stature and imposing in person, he, like so many other poor mortals, found it hard to give credit to others. So, although it is said that he once declined Commodore Conner's offer of heavy ordnance from the ships, yet he was now obliged to ask for the navy Columbiads which were to breach the walls and thus enable him to turn his face to the northwest and cry "Excelsior."

At last the signals from the flag-ship came. On March 21, shortly after that hoisting of the colors which takes place daily on every American fort and man-of-war, our naval world was electrified by the signal, "Commodore Perry commands the squadron." The two commodores, Conner, veteran of the war of 1812, representative of the past and the glories of the sailing ship, and Perry, the apostle of steam and the future diplomatist, to open Japan to the world, at once visited General Scott in his tent. There the commander-in-chief asked for the loan of six heavy navy guns to form a battery in the army. Instantly Perry replied, "Certainly, General, but I must fight them . . . wherever the guns go, the sailors go with them."

Scott declined. His vanity was wounded. He wanted his own soldiers to man the batteries; but "guns and men together" was Perry's rule. So Scott renewed the bombardment with his light field-pieces, only to find that he was wasting time. The shot could not penetrate or breach the walls. Swallowing his pride, he requested Perry to send the guns along with the sailors.

The Commodore in person got into his boat, and pulling round under the sterns of his war-ships, announced the order. Instead of scraping and scrubbing and acting as laborers, our jackies were once more to uphold the glorious prestige of the navy. Already the marines were doing duty in the trenches as part of the third artillery. The news thrilled the blue-jackets, and cheer after cheer went up from our ships.

It was Captain Robert E. Lee, one of the ablest American officers ever known on this continent, who built the naval battery, which in the circumvallation was *Number Four*. Made of sand-bags, with walls over six feet thick, it had traverses to resist a flanking or a raking fire from the castle. The guns were mounted on their own ship's carriages and set opposite the fort of Santa Barbara. The sailors worked the guns and the powder boys brought the ammunition from trenches in the rear, behind which the supporting infantry lay. Picked crews served two 32-pounders from the *Potomac* and the *Raritan*, and four 68-pounders from the *Mississippi*, the *Albany*, and the *St. Mary's*. These were called Paixhans or Columbiads, and were the most famous guns of the day. They could fire bombshells, which the old-style cannon could not. Not until it was finished and the guns mounted, did the Mexicans discover the naval battery, which had been built behind cover, masked by the dense chaparral or cane-brake, so common in Mexico and Texas, made of evergreen oak and thorny shrubs.

When our men found out, from the lively music of the Mexican cannon balls playing over their heads, that they had been discovered, they were as lively as the chaparral-cocks which live at home in the prickly undergrowth. Some daring volunteers at once sprang out of the embrasures and chopped away the brush. This unmasked the work, and soon the cross fire of seven forts converged on this one naval battery. The castle also sent big 10- and 13-inch shells flying over and around them, until Perry diverted its fire, as we shall see.

The Mexican engineers wished particularly to destroy this new earthwork, for they well knew that it was the heavy shot from this battery which would certainly breach the walls. Indeed, as soon as their inspectors picked up the solid 32-pounder shot and one of the unexploded 8-inch shells, they felt that the city must quickly fall. Their hope was therefore to dismount the guns, and knock the battery to pieces. They concentrated directly their heaviest cannon and best artillerists opposite the naval battery, and put in command a German officer named Holzinger. Yet, notwithstanding all they could do, the fort received very little injury. Captain Lee showed faith in his own work, by remaining in the redoubt during the fire. At half-past two, ammunition was exhausted, and the hot metal was allowed to cool. By this time fifty feet of the city walls had been cut away, and a breach thirty-six feet wide, big enough for a storming party to enter, had been made, while the thicker walls of the forts were "drilled like a colander."

A relief party from the ship, led by Captain Mayo, with fresh ammunition, reached the battery by sunset. Only the best sailors, picked from all the vessels, were allowed the honor of serving at the guns. All night long the bombardment was kept up from the mortars. At daylight the boatswain's silver whistle called our sailors to breakfast, after which another terrific straight-line bombardment began. So rapid and so steady was the fire, that between seven and eight it was necessary to stop and let the guns cool. From daybreak to 1 P.M., our shipmen sent over six hundred 8-inch shells and solid shot into or within the city walls. They silenced several forts and wrought terrific destruction, for the difference between bombs falling downward and shot fired on a level is like that between a broadside and a raking fire at sea. The longer range is so much more destructive, because it has a vastly greater area of damage. Beside several officers and men killed in the battery, a number of the sailors were wounded by the cactus spurs and thorns, and bits of sand bags. Before leaving his work, so handsomely done, Captain Mayo called his men to the ramparts to give three cheers and thus to draw the fire of the Mexican forts. But none came. All were silenced. So after thirteen hundred rounds from the naval battery and great breaches in the walls, which thus opened the city to assault, Captain Mayo mounted his horse at 2 P.M. and rode to the headquarters of the general commanding, to announce results. In his joy, Scott almost pulled Captain Mayo off his horse, thanking him and the navy, in the name of the army, for this day's work.

It was now arranged that three storming columns should be formed, — one of marines and sailors, one of regulars, and one of volunteers. The volunteers were to enter through the widest breach made by the navy guns. The others were to storm the gates and climb the walls. Having no other materials, the carpenters of the *Mississippi* sawed up the studding sail booms to make ladders. The white flag and signals of surrender precluded any necessity of the Americans showing their valor.

Meanwhile the navy had still further coöperated handsomely with the army. Seeing that the castle was training its guns to destroy, if possible, the naval battery, Perry ordered Tattnall, with the *Spitfire* and *Vixen*, to approach, and at the distance of eighty yards to open fire in order to divert the gunners from the naval battery. The plan succeeded admirably. Had the Mexicans been good artillerists, they could have blown the little steamers out of the water, but their shots vexed only the waves. After they had swung their heavy cannon round, but as soon as they had improved their range, Perry called off the saucy brace of " mosquito steamers," on which the sailors were being very much wetted by ball and shell, which splashed up the brine like geyser springs. Tattnall was rather disappointed to find hardly any one hurt. In the thrill of delight, while still on deck, he exclaimed, " Well, this shortens life, but it broadens it."

Unconditional and immediate surrender was the

only proposition made, and this was accepted. A terrible wind-storm, though there was bright moonlight, followed. Much to the surprise of General Scott the castle also surrendered, the moral effects of the naval battery being sufficient. Alvarado was soon after captured, furnishing our army with animals for transportation, so that General Scott was enabled to move up into the interior.

CHAPTER XX.

SCOTT'S ADVANCE TO THE CITY OF MEXICO.

UP to the time of the Mexican war the sailors of the United States navy had a great prejudice against being drilled as infantry. Operations on land by seamen, except in a very irregular way, had been very rare. With the coming in of steamers, where so much less toil is required in the handling of sails and ropes, and where most of the hoisting and other heavy work of the ship, formerly done with human muscle, is now accomplished by machinery, the situation was changed. The time was ripe to turn sailors into soldiers and to form a naval brigade, and the opportunity was well improved. Our blue-jackets are now so well drilled in the evolutions of infantry that in the parades and processions they show a handsome equality with our militiamen, not only in marching, but in evolutions and the manual of arms.

Commodore M. C. Perry was the first one to form a naval brigade. With ten pieces of artillery, twenty-five hundred men were thoroughly drilled, first to handle musket and bayonet, and then to move in company and battalion formation. While Scott was forcing the pass of Cerro Gordo, Perry's ships crossed the bar at the river's mouth, stormed the fort, and Tuspan was "taken at a gallop."

The next enterprise was to capture Tobasco. This was new work for United States sailors; for instead of ship-to-ship duels, boat expeditions or squadron fights in line, our sailors were to charge against infantry intrenched behind earthworks. With 1084 seamen and marines in forty boats, the ships towed the expedition seventy miles up a river covered on both sides with dense chaparral. With three cheers and a charge the men landed, formed, drew their howitzers up the hill, and marched on Tobasco. On the plain before the city they met the Mexican army, with two-field pieces and cavalry, commanded by General Bruno. Our artillery was first handsomely served, and then a charge put the Mexicans to flight. While the steamers poured their fire into Fort Iturbide, Lieutenant, afterward Admiral, Porter landed with sixty-eight men and captured the fort by assault, so that soon our men marched into the town, company front, the band playing "Yankee Doodle." During the six days' occupancy, the sailors showed that they could act like good soldiers on land as well as keep discipline aboard ship.

Thus beside furnishing the battery which laid low the walls of Vera Cruz, and released the army to march into the interior, the navy captured six cities with their fortresses and ninety-three cannon, all of which work was done on land, off deck, and beyond the usual sphere of naval operations. No wonder that when General Scott sent the flagstaffs conquered from the city and castle of Vera Cruz to the museum of West Point, Commodore Perry required that on the brass plates should be inscribed, not "Taken by the American army," but "Taken by the American army and navy."

Meanwhile, one of the most splendidly conducted scientific campaigns known in history went on under the presiding genius of General Scott. Our little army of twelve thousand men climbed up the Mexican mountains, and at the almost inaccessible pass of Cerro Gordo found the Mexicans too strongly intrenched to be attacked in front. Scott cut a road around the mountain, and on the 17th of April reached the Jalapa road, where he could strike Santa Anna in the rear. Early in the morning of the 18th, Scott ordered his men forward. With a furious rush, our blue-coats charged on the gayly uniformed Mexicans. Colonel Harney, taking some of his men, captured the tower, which was the key to the whole position; while General Pillow's division moved through a terrible musketry fire upon General Vega's force. Though driven back, they reformed and charged again with success, gathering in three thousand prisoners. In this battle our men lost four hundred and thirty-one, of whom sixty-three were killed. The Mexican army was routed. Five thousand stands of arms and forty-three pieces of artillery were taken. The result was the occupation of Jalapa, with its fine climate and splendid scenery, dominated by the snow-capped peak of Orizaba.

Many were the jokes cracked by our brave fellows, who had never seen the fair city or region of Jalapa. They remembered the nauseous purgative drug exported from this city, when "calomel and jalap" formed one of the favorite prescriptions of the doctors. Indeed, this was the period in which many "Dago" words and expressions grew up. Our volunteers used to sing in camp, "Green grow the rushes, O," and hence the name, in South America, of the North Americans as "Gringoes." This was also one of the first wars in which newspapers made some men famous and destroyed the reputation of others; for the war correspondent had already moved into American history and begun his career. General Taylor was called "Rough and Ready," and General Scott "Fuss and Feathers." Some of the sayings on the battlefield got to be very popular, such as "A little more grape, Captain

Bragg," "Wait, Charlie, till I draw their fire," and "Where the guns go, the men go with them."

Our banners now advanced into the beautiful province of Puebla. The country was noted for its richness in silver and other metals, and the lovely Mexican onyx with which we are all acquainted. On this highland region Scott's army spent the summer. Besides being reënforced, it was brought into a superb state of discipline. When, on the 7th of August, the cry "On to Mexico" was changed into a quickstep march, and our men set forward with cheers, Scott did not fear to meet an army twice the number of his own. On the 20th, fourteen miles from the city, the first one of three battles on the same day was fought and victory won. Although the Mexican troops showed stubbornness and bravery, they could not withstand the charges of our men. The line of battle moved off to Churubusco, six miles south of the city, where heavy fighting took place. Three thousand prisoners were taken and thirty-seven cannon were captured, our army losing by death and casualty 1053 men. The third fight on this eventful day completed the victory, the Americans keeping up the chase of the beaten foe almost to the very gates of the capital.

Then, instead of Scott's being able to move at once upon the city, to harvest the results of his victory, an armistice of fifteen days took place.

The war was stopped, as it were, by injunction, through a commissioner invited from Washington. Scott was thus left with his little army in the heart of the enemy's country, where his supplies and reënforcements could easily be cut off, while the Mexicans were able to recover and reorganize. Negotiations failed, however, and on the 7th of September Scott prepared to advance. On the 8th Worth's division of four thousand men captured Casamata, and also the fortification called Molino del Rey, or the King's Mill.

One tremendously strong fortress now remained. This was called Chapultepec, where was the military school of the Mexican republic. It stands on a strongly fortified hill, and an immense amount of money and skill had been spent to make the place impregnable. To mask his real purpose, Scott ordered two batteries of artillery to keep up a heavy fire, during September 12 and 13, which had the effect of drawing the enemy within the city walls. Meanwhile our engineers put up heavy batteries on the night of the 11th, which, during the two days following, directed their fire on the castle and outworks. Then on the 13th, at eight o'clock in the morning, under Captains McKenzie and Casey, two assaulting parties, of 260 men each, moved forward to the stronghold, while over their heads there fell upon the enemy from our batteries a rain of shot and shell. Over rocks, and chasms, and mines, and in the face of heavy fire of cannon and musketry, our men rushed forward, climbing up, without giving the Mexicans time to explode the mines laid in the ground. After the redoubt midway on the heights had been taken, our brave fellows reached the ditch and main wall of the work, putting scaling ladders up against the masonry. No sooner were the pioneers once inside than it looked as if a wave of blue were falling over the walls and mounting up the west side.

On the south side our men had to move across a causeway, and here the contest was desperate; but discipline and valor overcame every obstacle. Batteries and works were carried. Ever higher yet our soldiers moved forward, until they planted the stars and stripes at the highest point. During these three terrible days our army lost 863 men, but not stopping, they pressed on along the two causeways, and continued the fighting at the city gates. Scott would grant no terms, and the divisions of Worth and Quitman entered the capital. Although street fighting continued during two days, the position was held, and the city made secure. Scott had now less than six thousand troops.

After this decisive victory some occasional skirmishes took place, but the guerillas were more annoying than dangerous. The whole story of the

American army in Mexico is a magnificent tribute to the science, skill, and character of our generals; to the splendid discipline of our little army; to the moral stamina and intelligence of the American volunteer. The contrast between the ability of the officers and the discipline of the rank and file in the War of 1812 with that of 1846 is as great as one could imagine.

The Mexican soldiers were docile and brave, and were accustomed to stand in the ranks during the firing, calmly meeting death; but when the American troops made a rush and charge, they were unable to hold their ground. The United States soldier was not only stronger in body and a better fighting machine, but was a more intelligent person. He had had a public school education. He knew what he was fighting for. He could not only be brave, but he could keep up his courage and endure hardness, amid fatigue and danger during many hours. Many, perhaps most, of the city-bred men in the army were also members of the volunteer fire department at home. This, with all its faults, was an admirable school of alertness, intelligence, courage, discipline, and manliness. After standing up to heavy fighting, and shooting with an idea to serious business, our volunteers, when once they could start the Mexicans on the run, rapturously enjoyed the excitement. They found the chase in war to have more fun and exhilaration than if they were running to a fire or racing with a rival engine.

Nor was it difficult to account for the brilliancy of our victories, when it is also considered what splendid officers the American graduates of West Point were. These outgeneralled the Mexican leaders by exact science. General Worth well deserved the monument which the city of New York erected to his memory on Fifth Avenue, opposite Madison Square.

In the navy two great reforms begun and were soon carried out. One was the abolition of flogging and the other of the grog ration. Altogether, about 100,000 troops had been employed, of which 26,090 were regulars, 56,926 were volunteers, and over 15,000 in the navy or in the department of commissariat and transportation. About 120 officers and 1400 men fell in battle or died of wounds, and 100 officers and 10,800 men perished by disease; or, in round numbers, about 20,000 lives were lost, one-fourth by the casualties of war, and three-fourths by sickness. The total expense of the war was about $150,000,000; but this sum was vastly increased by pensions.

Buena Vista was Taylor's last battle, but he had won a victory not only over Santa Anna, but over the hearts of the American people, who are easily captured by military men. The name of the site of victory, from which General Taylor stepped into the presidential chair, was once unheard of in our country. It is now applied to over forty towns and villages in the United States.

Old "Rough and Ready" was the son of the colonel of a Virginia regiment in the Revolutionary War. He had spent most of his life on the frontier, among soldiers and Indians. He began his military life in 1804 as lieutenant of the seventh infantry, and had served in the Black Hawk and Florida wars. By his battle on Christmas Day, 1837, he had decisively beaten the Seminoles, and with Worth's diplomacy had virtually ended the Florida war. It is said that he had not voted for forty years. In the nominating convention his name ran ahead of those of Clay, Scott, and Webster.

In the election the popular vote for Taylor was 1,360,752. Cass and Butler, the Democratic candidates, had 1,219,962 votes. For Van Buren and Adams, the "free-soilers," only 291,342 ballots were cast. So the man of the camp was called to the service of the nation in the presidential chair. He was inaugurated March 4, 1849.

The country was now again called to face the problems of expansion, and great questions loomed up concerning the organization of the new territory. The forces of freedom and slavery were being arrayed in that terrific conflict of words which preceded the bloody struggle on the battlefield. Like the majority of purely military officers called to high civil posts, Taylor was destined to prove a failure as President. As a rule, the work of army officers in high civil administration contrasts pitifully with the achievements in the field. Usually the two records are like those of pygmy and giant. President Taylor was saved from further troubles by his death, which occurred July 9, 1850. Millard Fillmore, whose name was destined to be well known in Japan, became President.

By the treaty of Guadalupe Hidalgo, peace had been secured and New Mexico and California were ceded to the United States. Thus again the area of our country, by being increased one-third in size, was vastly enlarged. Nearly a million square miles of land, having over three thousand miles of seacoast, with three great harbors, came under the American flag.

And yet this great territory might have waited a long while for inhabitants, had it not been for what has been called the "accidental" discovery of some shining grains of gold. These were found on Captain Sutter's farm.

Do we call the discovery of gold in California an accident? Yet what is an accident? In Christendom, and especially in the United States, many wonderful inventions have been the result of happy "accidents." Yet such accidents do not occur in the middle of Africa, or among the Esquimaux, or the red Indians, and not often in countries where people are not educated to think, or where discovery is frowned upon and research is considered dangerous to religion or the government. Spaniards and Indians were in California, the latter thousands, and the former hundreds of years, but there were no such "accidents" as the finding of gold. When, however, trained Cornish miners came to California, they found at an unexpected moment what their habits of life taught them to look for.

When the news of this discovery went over the land and the world, the name "California," from having been a mere name in a romance, or a geographical expression for an obscure region, was transformed into an alluring image whose face reflected light and magnetism all over the earth. Immediately young men from the East, the returned volunteer, the hardy and venturous European from old lands across the sea, were attracted to the Pacific slope. With the "prairie schooner," slowly and painfully making their way across the great American desert, they thronged in caravans. Or they came in sailing vessels around Cape Horn; or took steamer, crossed the Isthmus, and again embarked and steamed up the coast. In four years two hundred and fifty thousand men of every sort of character, almost wholly without women and the refinements of life, were on the new El Dorado. Then began the digging and the washing, and the output of that volume of wealth which has surprised the world. Yet California's wealth from precious metals has been vastly less than that gained from tilling the soil. "The Argonauts of '49" found the true golden fleece in agriculture and not in mining.

Another cession of territory was made in 1853, when Mexico sold to our government for the sum of $10,000,000 that part of Arizona and New Mexico that lies south of the Gila River. This "Gadsden purchase," named from the negotiator, added to our national domain a strip of territory nearly as large as the state of New York, or 45,535 square miles.

CHAPTER XXI.

THE AMERICAN SAILOR IN THE FAR EAST.

OUR early war-ships on the East India station, which included at first the waters of China and Japan, were the old sailing frigates, sloops of war, or brigs. The first United States war steamer to get to the far East was the *San Jacinto*. She was named after the closing battle in the war of Texan independence, fought April 21, 1836, between General Houston and Santa Anna. In 1855 this vessel took out Townsend Harris, who made a treaty with Siam and one with Japan. This latter opened the empire to American residence and commerce.

While the *San Jacinto* was on the China station, the British and Chinese were having a quarrel which ended in war. The Chinese had built forts near Canton, to form a barrier that should hinder foreign vessels from coming up the river. The mandarins paid little or no attention, as they ought to have done, to the difference in the national ensigns. Although they themselves usually sent armies to the field with thousands of banners, streamers, and

even fans, umbrellas, and gongs,— things which are
nonsense when real fighting is to be done,— so that
the number as compared with the fighting men was
absurdly great, they had no real flag. They had
not yet reached that clear sense of nationality in
the world which would teach them to have a dis-
tinctive Chinese ensign of their own. Indeed, there
was no really national flag of Japan or Korea, until
contact with western nations compelled these people to make one. In the pride and conceit of her-
mits, each thought his country the centre of the
universe and other people barbarians. Each nation
has now a national standard.

So it happened that when American ships, which,
being perfectly neutral, had a right to pass the barrier forts, were fired upon, it was time to teach the
Chinese mandarins the rights of neutrals and the
laws of war. Commodore Armstrong could not get
his flag-ship, the *San Jacinto*, into the shallow river,
so he ordered Captain Foote, who afterward was
Admiral and commanded the gunboats on the Mississippi, to go up the river, bombard, capture, and
destroy the Chinese fort. The *Portsmouth* was a
sailing ship, and had to be towed by the little
American steamer *Willamette*. The *Levant*, an
old wooden war-ship, was pulled up by the steam-
launch *Kum Fa*, but she struck on a rock and could
not fight that day. The Chinese opened at once

with grape and round shot, but after the *Portsmouth* got into position, her 8-inch guns began to knock the granite blocks of the largest and lowest fort out of their places, while her shells burst inside the walls with terrific effect. By evening the fort was almost silent.

After several days of unavailing diplomacy, a land attack was ordered. Four hundred of our marines and sailors in boats towed by the *Kum Fa* were landed at the edge of a rice-field. Then, with ladders, axes, carbines, and cutlasses, they charged upon the gates of the fort. Besides their jingal balls the Chinese fired rockets made of bamboo poles armed with an iron spear-head and feathered at the ends. The clumsy missiles made a terrible wound when they hit any one; but both their cannon and jingal balls flew over our men's heads and their bamboo rocket arrows went hissing and bouncing over the fields like Fourth-of-July chasers. While our men were charging, the *Levant* and *Portsmouth* kept up their cannonade, but both ships ceased firing as soon as the Americans entered within the fort. Then the garrison broke and fled. Of the 176 guns captured within the walls, one was an 8-inch bronze piece weighing fifteen tons.

This was one of the bravest exploits of our men abroad, and the seven men killed in the battle are commemorated in the monument at the Brooklyn

Navy Yard. It was easy to recall their story, when in July, 1898, just before going to Europe, I visited the *Portsmouth* lying as the receiving-ship in the Hudson River at Hoboken. The *Portsmouth* in her day was a fine sailer and in every way a useful ship.

Our old friend Commodore Josiah Tattnall, whom we last saw in front of the castle at Vera Cruz, came out to Chinese waters in 1860. In the chartered steamer *Toeywan* (another name for Formosa) he was to carry the American minister, Mr. Ward, into the Peiho River, which is up in the north of China and leads past Tientsin to the capital. The British and French were at war with the Chinese, who built forts in a line, and below and above had stretched heavy booms of wood held together with iron chains and staples. In the attack, the allied fleet of thirteen gunboats, under Admiral Hope, blew up one boom and bombarded the fort, but they were unable to force or blow up the upper barrier of timber and iron. In fact, being caught in the narrow river under the short-range fire of the heavy guns of the Chinese forts, several of their ships were sunk. On others, the gun crews were all killed and wounded. About four hundred and thirty men had been struck down, and the situation was dreadful. Even on the flag-ship *Plover*, only the bow gun was being served.

Commodore Tattnall standing on deck outside the bar, glass in hand, was a witness of this awful spectacle. He stood it as long as he could. Then crying out, "Blood is thicker than water," he ordered the ship's cutter. He passed, like Perry on Lake Erie, through the thickest of the fight, as his men pulled oar toward the British commander's ship. A Chinese cannon ball tore into the stern of the cutter, killed the coxswain, and narrowly missed sinking the boat with all on board. Ranging up alongside, Tattnall leaped on board and offered the use of his surgeons for the wounded of the fleet.

While their commander was thus occupied, his boat's crew of American sailors jumped on board the *Plover*, relieved the British sailors, who were utterly exhausted, and served the gun. Our men fired a round or two at the Chinese fort, and then Tattnall, though he hated to do it, ordered his men off. There was a growl in his voice, put on for official purposes, but there was no disapproval in his twinkling eyes. Afterward, in the land expedition, Tattnall helped to tow boatloads of British marines in action to storm the forts.

It is an old Scotch proverb that says, "Blood is warmer than water." Tattnall gave it his own or the English form, and made it "thicker." His action, although technically a violation of international law, must be excused when it is remembered that the Chinese at that time did not care anything about the laws of nations, and that the American Commodore offered the services of his surgeons to the Chinese also, which they declined. The Chinese have never been very much interested in saving the lives of their men wounded in battle. Even in 1894 they went to war with Japan without a hospital corps. Until Christian sentiments prevail in China, they are not likely to furnish surgeons, hospitals, and nurses to their soldiers.

In Japan large squadrons flying the stars and stripes have gathered more than once, but for peaceful purposes, and to perform those acts which have bound Columbia and the Mikado's empire in permanent peace and mutual regard. Commodore Matthew C. Perry, in July, 1853, with the United States steamships *Mississippi* and *Susquehanna* and the United States ships *Plymouth* and *Saratoga*, entered the bay of Yedo, and delivered the President's letter of friendship. In March, 1854, he came again, and at Yokohama, Perry, the sailor-diplomatist, and the professor-statesman Hayashi, made the treaty which begun the modern intercourse of Japan with the world. Townsend Harris, our first Consul-general, after many months of patient instruction of the hermit-statesman in Yedo, and later assisted by Commodore Tattnall, obtained a more liberal treaty, in 1858, which secured trade and residence of Americans at five ports and in two cities. Thus did our peaceful diplomacy win the friendship and respect of a proud-spirited people, and the most progressive nation in Asia — " the rudder of the whole continent."

When the daimio of Choshiu erected batteries on the bluffs commanding the narrow strait of Shimonoséki, tried to close the Inland Sea, and fired on the American ship *Pembroke*, Captain David MacDougal, in the United States corvette *Wyoming*, then in search of the *Alabama*, steamed into the straits, July 16, 1862, and there performed one of the most brilliant and daring feats in the annals of the United States navy. He engaged five batteries and silenced one. He ran his ship between two armed vessels, fought both and sunk one. Then manœuvring into position, he sent an 11-inch shell into the boiler of the large war steamer, blowing her up and sinking her, again fighting the batteries on his return. In this battle of seventy minutes, the *Wyoming* fired fifty-five rounds, or, from the time of actual firing, one a minute. Struck in twenty places, the ship, though losing four killed and six wounded, came out in good trim.

In 1864, the allied British, French, and Dutch and American squadrons bombarded the forts, now increased to ten, and completely destroyed them. Our flag was represented by Lieutenant Pearson, with a Parrott rifle gun and thirty marines and sailors, on the chartered steamer *Ta Kiang*, in a manner to win the admiration of the admiral commanding. Then the alert and progressive Japanese took the matter to heart and concluded first to imitate, and then excel, the foreigners, and join in the race of modern civilization.

As nobly patriotic and efficient at the ends of the earth as in American waters, our navy has always sustained the honor of the nation. Shimonoséki was the precursor of Manila. Cool, scientific, brave, and bold, MacDougal, in 1862, set a mark for Dewey at Manila in 1898.

CHAPTER XXII.

CONFEDERATES AND FEDERALS.

THE battle over slavery was fought on the floor of Congress, before its theatre was transferred to the open field. One party at the North believed slavery to be a curse. Another party at the South looked upon it as a blessing. The pulpit, the press, and political economy were divided, as the country was.

Even the religious denominations of the country were rent asunder, but the Reformed, the Congregational, the Episcopal, and the Roman Catholic churches maintained their unity. The longer the debate, the hotter grew the spirit of the disputants. Texas was the last one admitted as a slave state, but California came in free.

All compromises were in vain. One party cried "no more slave states." Another said that negroes were property, and every citizen of the United States could take what was his own, including his black slaves, with him. A third part denied the right of Congress to decide the question of free or slave states, declaring that the people of the territories were the sovereigns.

Many blacks escaped from bondage into the free states. Congress passed a law allowing slave owners to secure the fugitives. When these attempted to do so, there were riots and rescues. I well remember some of these in Philadelphia. In many places, especially in Pennsylvania, New York, and Ohio, kind-hearted persons helped the black people to get privately to Canada. By day they fed and sheltered the fugitives in barns and cellars. When it was dark, they convoyed them from one town to another, or showed them the way. Thus these pilgrims of the night followed the north star to freedom under the British flag. Quiet, secret, effective, was "the underground railroad" to Canada.

Mr. Seward declared that we had on hand an "irrepressible conflict," and Mr. Lincoln said that no nation could exist half slave and half free. There was much talk, which greatly scared some parsons and many persons, about "a higher law" as being above acts of Congress. Then came the publication of the novel "Uncle Tom's Cabin," which showed both the bright and the dark side of slavery. This book sold by hundreds of thousands and roused the popular sentiment, educating millions to a hatred against the bondage of the blacks.

When Clay, Webster, and Calhoun died, as they did before 1852, new men like Thaddeus Stevens and Charles Sumner, on the one hand, and Jeffer-

son Davis and John C. Breckenridge on the other,
took their places in Congress. The Missouri Compromise of 1820, which shut out slavery from the
territory north and west of Missouri, was repealed.
This precipitated a great struggle for the possession of Kansas. Should it be settled by free men
or slaveholders? Soon there were rival governments on the soil, and for five years the territory
was torn by civil war. Border ruffians and abolitionists fought each other, and not a little blood
was shed; but Kansas finally entered the Union
without slavery.

Two days after President James Buchanan had
been inaugurated, the Supreme Court of the
United States under Chief Justice Taney decided
that negro slaves were not "persons," notwithstanding that the Constitution speaks of them as
such, but were simply pieces of property having
no rights which white men were bound to respect.
Therefore slaves could be taken into free territory, the same as horses or cattle.

In the midst of the increasing hostilities between
the sections north and south, came the financial
panic of 1857. This was followed, however, by the
discovery of silver in Nevada, of petroleum in
Pennsylvania, and, later, of lead and silver in Colorado and Utah, and of natural gas in western Pennsylvania. Then ensued the episodes of the John

Brown raid at Harper's Ferry, and the election to the presidency of Abraham Lincoln. By the 1st of February, 1861, seven states had seceded from the Union. At Montgomery, Alabama, they took the name of the Confederate States of America. Fort Sumter was attacked and surrendered. President Lincoln issued his call for 75,000 volunteers to suppress the rebellion. By the middle of June, four more states having seceded, there were eleven in the Confederacy.

The population of the Union at this time was about 32,000,000, of whom 23,000,000 were in the states loyal to the Constitution, while in the Confederacy were 6,500,000 white men and about 3,500,000 slaves. The Confederates had the advantage of plenty of arms and ammunition which they had seized, and a majority not only of the best-known officers in the regular army, but perhaps also of the navy. They had also the benefit of resources in labor, by which an army in the field could be fed by unpaid toilers at home. There was an immense advantage in fighting for defence and on their own soil. On the other hand they had few factories and very little skilled labor. For the making of an ironclad war vessel, the ore must first be blasted, dug, smelted, refined, and rolled. The raw materials for the making of powder and campaign supplies must be first provided. Reliance must be placed upon Europe for nearly all manufactured articles. Payment could be made in cotton through the blockade runners.

The resources of the North in money, materials, factories, mills, founderies, and shipyards were very great. There were twice as many men, and labor was in honor. With command of the sea and the power to obtain a large navy, the government could blockade the southern ports and cut off supplies from Europe. Yet, in the summer of 1861, the Union force was but little larger than those of the Confederacy. General Scott directed one army and General Beauregard the other. The Union line, between Fortress Monroe and Harper's Ferry, was called "the Army of the Potomac." The "Army of Northern Virginia" was the name given to the Confederate force, which had Richmond as its centre. There were also opposing forces in Missouri and West Virginia and in the southwest. The Confederates held the Mississippi River from New Orleans to Columbus and hoped to control Kentucky, beside holding the Tennessee and Cumberland rivers.

The battle of Bull Run served only to arouse the North to greater efforts. Congress voted to raise a half million men and half a billion dollars to carry on the war. General George B. McClellan was put in command of the Army of the Potomac.

By his continuous labors and after six months of steady drill, he had made it the splendid fighting machine which it was and through all its vicissitudes remained. The plan of campaign, elaborated in Washington, was first to blockade the seaports of the Confederacy, to take Richmond, to open the rivers of the southwest, and to march a Union army from the Mississippi to the Atlantic Ocean.

The contrary plan, elaborated in Richmond, was defence on land and aggression at sea. A fleet of privateers and commerce-destroyers, among which were the *Alabama*, *Florida*, *Shenandoah*, *Rappahannock*, *Georgia*, and *Tallahassee*, was let loose on the oceans. Their success was so great that the commerce of the United States was wiped off the seas. Americans dwelling in foreign lands felt like men without a country.

In November, 1861, Messrs. Mason and Slidell were sent as envoys of the Confederacy to obtain recognition abroad, but Captain Wilkes, the famous explorer, stopped the British mail steamer *Trent* and took them as prisoners. Yet the very thing that the American commander had done was what we had protested against for fourscore years. When, therefore, the British government demanded that the prisoners be given up, Mr. Seward, our able Secretary of State, at once released them. Thus our government showed that consistency which is so precious a jewel. In Europe the two envoys accomplished little or nothing. Even Mr. Edward A. Freeman, who started to write a book, entitled "The History of Federal Government from the Amphictyonic Council to the Disruption of the United States of America," published but one volume. Then the victories of the Union armies compelled indefinite postponement of the book.

The efforts of the Confederates to build, float, and equip a navy were extraordinary. Seizing the Norfolk Navy Yard, they turned the old *Merrimac* into an ironclad. It had sloping sides, and its plating was chiefly of railroad material. Although a very shaky craft, the new monster, riding on the old hulk, was able to move out against the grand old wooden frigates *Cumberland* and *Congress*, then lying opposite Fortress Monroe. These were rammed and sunk in a few minutes, their broadsides rattling on and rebounding from the dented but unpierced iron sides of the *Merrimac*.

On Sunday, March 9, a new oddity, the *Monitor*, appeared. She looked to the Confederates like a "tomato can upon a shingle." A duel took place, and the *Merrimac* went back to her quarters. The *Monitor* could not be hurt. This little event dictated the reconstruction of all the navies of the world. From this time forth wood, as a material for war vessels, was obsolete. In our days of steel battle-ships, even the libraries of books, the sailors' bags, clothes, hammocks, and everything combustible are thrown overboard, lest they take fire in battle.

The war of power between guns and penetrating missiles, armor and power of resistance, goes on in our day just as it went on in the Middle Ages. At first leather and hide-covered shields were sufficient. Then followed chain mail and scale armor; but when the arrows were made longer and heavier and the bows stronger, chain and scale armor gave way to plates riveted together, and this in turn to ugly and clumsy boxes of iron, that made men look as if they were dressed up in ash cans and coal scuttles. Men thickened their coats of defence, clothing themselves more and more in hardware, until the knights were so heavy that they had to be helped to get on their horses. When they fell off, they lay helpless as turtles turned upside down.

By and by, in the final evolution of force from the stone-headed arrow, the bullet came into play, which no amount of steel which a man is able to wear can resist; armor was dropped and became only a curiosity. So in time will it be with ship armor. Admiral Dupont, when he saw how life was made so uncomfortable to the fighters in the monitors, longed for iron men to fight in these metal ships, which were more like junk-shops or dry docks than the beautiful, full-sailed, and majestic sailers of old times. During the war most of the best work of blockade and battle had to be done necessarily by the wooden frigates and gunboats, but new monitors were quickly built and launched, and they served nobly to reduce fortresses. In one of them, the *Weehawken*, Captain John Rodgers, with consummate coolness and skill, fought and sunk, within fifteen minutes, the ironclad *Atlanta* in Savannah harbor. This event took place just fifty years after the conflict between the *Chesapeake* and *Shannon* in Boston harbor, and finely illustrated the progress made in naval science during a half century.

The line of defence of the Confederacy was first broken in the west by the capture of Forts Henry and Donelson. This was brought about by Commodore Foote with his gunboats and by General Grant with his army, compelling the surrender of fifteen thousand prisoners, which up to that time was the greatest number ever taken in any battle on this continent. After the great battle at Shiloh, or Pittsburg Landing, in which twenty-five thousand men were killed or wounded, Commodore Foote captured Island Number Ten, which opened the Mississippi River all the way to Vicksburg. One of the popular songs of the war was, "Ho, for the Gunboats, Ho!"

The next year Farragut, with fifty wooden vessels, moved up the Mississippi. New Orleans was defended by Forts Jackson and Philip, by heavy chain cables stretched across the stream, and by fifteen armed vessels, including two ironclads. Farragut was assisted by Butler's land forces and Commodore Porter's bomb boats which rained 300-pounder shells into the forts. The advancing Union fleet silenced the guns, broke the cables, and sunk the ships. Once more the stars and stripes floated on the public buildings of New Orleans. Port Hudson and Vicksburg remained to contest and prevent the desired meeting of the sea-going fleet of Farragut with the river gunboats of Foote.

In the east, McClellan, leaving a hundred thousand men in Washington, marched with another hundred thousand through the peninsula between the James and the York rivers to the southeast of Richmond, where weeks were spent in fighting malaria, mud, weather, and water. There were heavy battles at Seven Pines and Fair Oaks and opposition at Williamsburg and Yorktown. When General Robert Lee took command of the Confederate forces, he despatched Stonewall Jackson to drive out the Union forces from the Shenandoah Valley and General Stuart to make a raid in the rear of McClellan's army, and both were very successful. The armies of Fremont, Banks, and McDowell were united under the name of the Army of Virginia, and General John Pope was made their commander. Toward the end of June, after heavy fighting, during what has been called the Seven Days' Battle, culminating at Malvern Hill, the Army of the Potomac retreated to the James River and afterward fell back nearer Washington. After the loss of thirty thousand men, matters on both sides stood as they had been before. When President Lincoln called for fresh volunteers, the shout went up all over the Union, "We are coming, Father Abraham, three hundred thousand more," and they came.

A second terrific battle was fought at Bull Run, in which Pope, confronted by Stonewall Jackson, was badly defeated. Most of the Federal troops retreated to their fortifications at Washington. General Lee crossed the Potomac above Washington, expecting that the Marylanders would rise up and march with him. At Harper's Ferry Jackson captured the Union garrison with plenty of arms and stores. McClellan, advancing to Sharpsburg against Lee, fought the bloody battle at Antietam, with a loss of twenty-six thousand men. Lee was compelled to retreat. McClellan was superseded by Burnside, who, setting out to march on Richmond, crossed the Rappahannock River and attacked the Confederate fortifications, but was driven back with terrible loss, and General Joseph Hooker was given the command of the army in the east. In this month of December, a battle was fought at Murfreesboro, Tennessee, between the armies of Generals Bragg and Rosecrans, lasting three days, and ending in the advantage of the Union army. Thus the year closed.

CHAPTER XXIII.

THE WAR FOR FREEDOM.

ON the first of January, 1863, the Emancipation Proclamation changed the character of the war from one for the Union to one for freedom. During the first four months of 1863 little could be done except in the way of preparation, but when the Army of the Potomac moved, the Confederates met them at Chancellorsville, where a two days' battle was fought. The Union army was beaten. Yet this was the last triumph which the Confederates in Virginia won in the open field. Here they met with their greatest loss, for Stonewall Jackson was accidentally shot by his own men. After this no more victories came to the stars and bars.

General Lee was a statesman as well as a soldier. To save the Confederacy, he resolved to invade the free states and to conquer peace in a northern city. In June he "marched over the mountain wall" with about seventy thousand men, but at Gettysburg, General Meade, the Pennsylvanian, met him. Years before, a British officer visiting this valley plain, with Seminary Ridge on one side and Cemetery Ridge nearly opposite, had remarked on the fitness of the site for a great battle.

On July 1, 1863, the terrific struggle began, the Confederates at first getting the advantage. On the third day, General Pickett, with fifteen thousand men, the flower of the Confederate army, after a terrific cannonade of the Union forces, charged across a mile of open ground and up the slope of Cemetery Ridge. Then the Federal artillery opened upon them, first with round shot, then with shell, and finally with grape and canister. Yet on the brave Confederates moved, piercing the Union lines, but only to have the Federals close upon them, "gathering in flags by the sheaves and prisoners by the thousands," and driving back the fragments. Being on Pennsylvania soil, the Keystone State's own troops appropriately took a prominent part. In this most stubbornly contested battle of the war nearly fifty thousand men were killed or wounded. This was the high-water mark of the slaveholders' rebellion. The rest of the work of the Union armies and navies, heavy as it proved to be, was but the finishing of the task.

As I write this story, I remember well being at Camp Curtin, in Harrisburg, as a member of Company H of the 44th (Merchants') Regiment, Pennsylvania Volunteers, having heard the news of the battle of Gettysburg and received orders to march southward. We were to guard the fords of the Potomac after Lee's retreat. Governor Andrew Curtin came into the camp and went through it, announcing the fall of Vicksburg. Before leaving Philadelphia, I had been solemnly assured by some, especially by two venerable and famous friends of southern birth, that Vicksburg was impregnable. With battery rising above battery on the bluffs of the riverside, and bristling with heavy guns and an ample garrison in fortifications of the first order of scientific construction, it was impossible for an army to capture and occupy it.

As Governor Curtin went through the camp the men of the various counties came out to greet him. There were the stalwart lumbermen from Pike, Wayne, and Susquehanna counties, the coal miners of Schuylkill, Carbon, and Lehigh counties, the farmers from Bucks, Montgomery, and Chester counties, the sugar makers of Clinton, Union, and Lycoming counties, the sturdy "Pennsylvania Germans" from Lancaster, Lebanon, and York counties, the iron workers of Allegheny and Westmoreland counties, the boat and lake men from Erie and Crawford counties, — each delegation cheering and welcoming the governor of the commonwealth. Thus did the boy of nineteen get his first clear and full impression of an American state, with its counties and townships.

General Grant's forces had beaten those of Pemberton and Johnson, while the Federal artillery bombarded the city day and night. Food had become so scarce in Vicksburg that it was a question whether the wolf or the olive branch would get inside first. With marvellous courage and endurance, the Confederates held out until July 4. Then the army and the city surrendered. Five days later, Port Hudson followed the example. Then the mighty river was open from its source to the sea. Perry's old steam frigate the *Mississippi* grounded under fire of the batteries and was burned.

Two "fires in the rear" now disturbed the Union cause. One was an outburst of ruffianism in the city of New York, when rioters tried to resist the draft. After burning a negro orphan asylum, the cowards melted away at the appearance of the famous Sixth Corps of veterans. In Tennessee, Kentucky, Indiana, and Ohio, Morgan's Confederate cavalry made a destructive raid, only to be finally captured and destroyed.

In the battle of Chickamauga in September, Bragg defeated Rosecrans, though General Thomas saved the day. For two months the Union army was besieged by Bragg in Chattanooga. Late in November, when Hooker and Sherman came to command, they fought a battle above the clouds, driving the Confederates from Lookout Mountain and Missionary Ridge. The Confederates fled to Dalton, Georgia. Their cause was further weakened by General Sherman's raid into Mississippi.

On the 3d of March, 1864, General U. S. Grant was made commander-in-chief of all the Union armies. In the plan of campaign arranged with Sherman, it was decided that Grant should move against Lee and Richmond, while Sherman should defeat Johnson and march to the sea. The two Union armies were to unite near Richmond.

The last bloody and decisive campaign which sent the Confederacy to oblivion, gave us a united country able to face the world. Grant began his advance May 4. In the region of country called the Wilderness were fought indecisive battles, which, however, weakened the Confederates. The conflicts in the Wilderness were almost exclusively fought by infantry and with bullets, for both cavalry and artillery were nearly useless. Indeed, these were the most terrible musketry battles known in the history of the world. Grant then moved by the left flank southward, where at Cold Harbor he hurled his men upon the enemy's intrenchments and lost over ten thousand men within an hour, inflicting also great loss.

Finding himself unable to take the direct line of advance against the elaborate fortifications of Richmond, Grant moved round southward to Petersburg. At once both armies dropped sword and musket and began with pick and spade. Two grand lines of fortification, a comparatively short distance apart, were constructed. Beside a line of ditches and embankments, with bomb proofs, embrasures, and flanking guns, there were covered roads by which the men of either army in the reserve camps could reach their casemates. There were also regularly constructed forts at intervals along the line of forty miles or so, and a terrific and wasteful bombardment was kept up a large part of the time. During the whole campaign one battery on the right of the Union line, "the Petersburg Express," sent a shell every fifteen minutes, day and night, into various parts of the Confederate fortifications. Thus the winter passed away. In June, 1864, came news of the sinking of the *Alabama* by the *Kearsarge*.

To divert Grant's attention, weaken his force, and make him relax his grip, Lee sent General Early with a division of veterans to menace Washington. This able general got within five miles of the capital's fortifications. The Sixth Corps was sent up the Potomac and was personally met in Washington by Mr. Lincoln. Getting out in the open fields beyond the lines of defence, they drove Early off, after he had helped himself freely to the cattle and horses of the Maryland farmers. In return,

General Grant in August sent Sheridan into the Shenandoah Valley, with a force of Union cavalry, to destroy everything that could furnish food. The "granary of the Confederacy" was so utterly wasted that "if a crow wanted to fly the length of the valley he must take his rations with him." To-day, some of the most picturesque ruins in Virginia, covered with the creeper and the trumpet-flower vines, are memorials of the ruin wrought by Grant's orders.

In the Union army were mechanics of all kinds. Every trade and craft was represented. A study of the various regiments was very interesting, because the difference in the ways of doing things, of beginning or getting at a problem and solving it, varied so greatly among the different regiments. According as the majority of men, in each one, might be fishermen, shoemakers, lumbermen, machinists, farmers, clerks, cowboys, or miners, did habits and methods differ. In one of the Pennsylvania regiments was a large number of coal miners. They were as much used to burrowing under ground as are moles or rats. From them came the suggestion of digging an underground gallery and of making a mine under the Confederate fortifications, by which a fort could be blown up and a breach made, so that the Union forces could rush in, pierce the centre, divide and capture Lee's army.

To discover the site of the mine, of which they

learned from deserters, the Confederates went to the great trouble of sinking many shafts or pits in the tough clay, but they could not find the subterranean chamber. Meanwhile the Pennsylvanians burrowed under ground and placed four thousand pounds of powder in the chamber. Then, after lighting a time-fuse, preparations were made to assault. But through misunderstanding the whole affair was mismanaged. After the engineering work had been well done and the mines sprung, the explosion blew up a company of men, horses, and guns, making a breach several hundred feet long, which was called "the crater." The wary Confederates, having been warned beforehand, rushed so quickly to the repulse that hundreds of Union men were slaughtered in the hole, and others made prisoners.

Sheridan, after long and careful preparation, moved on Early's force in the Shenandoah Valley, and several battles were fought. While the general was away, the Union army was surprised at Cedar Creek, and getting into a panic were badly driven by the Confederates and had their camps looted. General Crook re-formed the Union forces, and Sheridan, arriving from Winchester, the battle turned to a victory. Indeed, Crook was a powerful intellectual force and one of the hardest fighters in Sheridan's army. To him much of the credit

MARCH TO THE SEA.

of this triumph, and not a little in other victories of Sheridan's, is due.

Meanwhile, Sherman had been marching from Chattanooga to Atlanta, where the chief railway centre and factories of the Confederacy were. Battles were fought at Resaca, Dallas, and Kenesaw Mountain. Yet neither opposing armies, nor the roughness of the hilly country, nor the steady downpour of rain during three weeks, nor the burning of bridges and tearing up of railways by the retreating Confederates, checked the Union advance. Sherman's men fought, built, relaid, and destroyed. Like a vast mowing machine, cutting a swath of destruction sixty miles wide, the Union army moved onward. Though he had lost thirty thousand men, Sherman captured Atlanta, burning all public buildings that contributed in any way to keep up the war. It was hoped in Richmond that Sherman would have to turn back in order to help Thomas, who was being pressed by General Hood; but leaving "the Rock of Chickamauga" to take care of himself, Sherman set out with his face toward the sea, two hundred miles distant. For a month nobody in the North heard anything from him. The slow and sure Thomas in mid-December attacked General Hood, demolished his army, and ended the war in the Southwest. On the 22d of December Sherman from Savannah wrote to President Lincoln, offering him as a Christmas gift the city of Savannah, with one hundred and fifty heavy guns, plenty of ammunition, and twenty-five thousand bales of cotton. On the 1st of February, after a month's rest, Sherman set his face northward, making a seven weeks' march through mud, rain, and swamp, besides fighting a battle at Goldsboro. On March 27, at City Point, Virginia, he and General Grant shook hands.

Meanwhile, Farragut and his fleet attacked Mobile. The Confederates, using torpedoes, blew up and rendered useless the monitor *Tecumseh*. Furthermore they had the *Tennessee*, an ironclad, commanded by Captain Franklin Buchanan, who had also fought the *Merrimac*. It was built of materials which only a few months before had been timber in the forest and ore in the ground. Yet Farragut did not hesitate to attack the forts and ironclads, and even to ram and try to sink the iron monsters with his wooden ships. After a heavy battle in August, he was victorious over all opposition, and sealed up the port of Mobile while the army garrisoned the city.

Like the constricting coils of an anaconda, the Union armies now closed on General Lee's forces. Sheridan moved down the Shenandoah Valley, cut the railroads and canals from Lynchburg, cutting off supplies from the West, and the next day moved further southward. While Lee was thus occupied with Sheridan, Grant ordered an advance along the whole line, capturing Petersburg, and compelling Lee to retreat from Richmond, which was soon occupied by our forces. Then driving forward the fragments of a once great army, he secured Lee's surrender at Appomattox Court House. There generous terms were made and food was immediately distributed to the hungry. Five days afterward, on the same day that the Confederates had won their first victory, Major Anderson hoisted over Fort Sumter the very same flag he had lowered four years before. Thus ended the war that had cost a half a million of lives, and probably $5,000,000,000. On some days the expenses of the United States government were over $3,500,000 a day.

CHAPTER XXIV.

A UNITED COUNTRY.

TWO magnificent pageants, the one material and the other moral, were witnessed at the end of the war. For the first time since 1861 the armies of the East and of the West made one host in Washington. On May 23 and 24, 1865, Pennsylvania Avenue presented a spectacle, the like of which had never before been seen on the American continent. In a column thirty miles long, the bronzed war veterans marched from the capitol up Pennsylvania Avenue past the Treasury Department, the reviewing stand where the President and his Cabinet stood, and the White House. Magnificent the display of Sheridan's thirteen thousand cavalry, ponderous the rumbling of three hundred pieces of artillery, funny beyond all telling the sight of Sherman's "bummers," wonderful the array of the pontoon train, pathetic the eloquence of the torn battle flags, and brilliant the sheen from miles of bayonets as the sunbeams played upon them!

I remember, when as a student preparing for college, how with my tutor I took the night boat

from Philadelphia down the Delaware River to
Baltimore. Then, by early train, we reached Washington. I saw the morning set her crown of
light upon the white dome of the capitol, in the
great space fronting which the veterans of the
Western armies were already gathering. These
men had hewn their way with their swords down
the Mississippi Valley, crossed Tennessee to Atlanta, marched eastward till they sniffed the salt air
of Savannah, and then pressed northward till they
joined their comrades of the Army of the Potomac.
I remember how I was impressed while looking at
Sherman, with his splendid staff of division officers,
and in hearing them talk.

I recall especially Custer, "the boy general with
the golden locks," who led his regiments of cavalry
which had, in every file, thirty horses breast to
breast, nostril to nostril, and hoof to hoof, moving forward and keeping dressed with wonderful precision,
while their riders in blue held the bridles in their
left hand and their flashing sabres in the other.
The young general, riding a fiery spotted mustang,
wore a sombrero or wide-brimmed Western prairie
hat that flared up in front, showing his broad white
forehead. The column had turned to the right at
the head of Fourteenth Street. A lady stepped
out from the sidewalk with a large wreath of
flowers, which she was about to put over the mus-

tang's neck or the general's, — I could not tell which, — but this wild Western pony, unused to such attentions, leaped forward as if shot out of a cannon. The general's hat fell off, but he did not. Not even a bucking or a rearing broncho could disturb his firm seat. Yet unexpected and in advance of time, to the surprise of the presidential party who could not understand the reason, the hatless general reined up his horse firmly, bowed, and rode back. Soon his troopers were with him, and his hat was on for a profound bow to the President when next he appeared. On the field of battle Custer was accustomed to ride ahead of his men toward the foe, and, gallantly making his bow to those he was about to fight, to ride back to join his troops and lead their charge. To his own men the episode seemed a natural one.

Glorious as the grand review at Washington was, the moral pageant was even more impressive. Within a few weeks the Union armies of the republic, which had put over two millions of men into the field, were disbanded. The American soldiers both North and South handed back their muskets and equipments of war and went to their home and work. Confederate and Federal alike took up the tools of peaceful livelihood. As wonderfully as in fiction Roderick Dhu's band, or in mythology Cadmus's armed dragon's-teeth warriors, the uniformed hosts of armed men melted away. Noble is the record of almost absolute freedom from lawlessness made by the men both of the blue and the gray.

After a few years the Grand Army of the Republic was formed of the veterans of the land and naval forces, and "posts" were established in most of the states, while the men of the gray uniform formed "camps." This was done for mutual friendship and assistance, for the joys of memory and the pleasures of oratory and feasting, and the inculcation of patriotism. It became the custom throughout the Union to decorate the graves of comrades with flowers. In time, all soldiers who had served their state or country in the field, and all sailors under the flag at sea of every war, were remembered. In later years Confederates and Federals marched together to make floral tribute to the brave. Thus the beautiful institution, the "American festival" of Decoration Day, now celebrated in all lands and on all seas, became fixed.

All this, with the formation of various other patriotic fraternities, for women as well as men, gave a tremendous impulse to the study of American history and to the marking, by tablets and other monuments, of the historic sites and spots in our great cities, towns, and even in our villages. In churches and halls, and wherever men gather, the deeds of the brave are commemorated. The United States government began the laying out of national cemeteries for the care and in honor of those who died for their country. Near all the great battlefields, ample plots of ground were selected, planted with trees, beautiful flowers, and shrubbery, and made lovely and attractive with eloquent emblems. Over each burial plot the government has set a neat, plain monument, or marking stone of white marble, with name, dates, military allocation, or has had chiselled the simple word "unknown." On the battlefields, the scars of which "nature has long since healed and reconciled to herself with the sweet oblivion of flowers," private munificence and national, state, or municipal enterprise have reared hundreds of memorials in art, making these once bloody fields gardens of beauty.

Gradually the passions of the war cooled. Hatred and bitterness died out. The "march of years" meant also the march of a great host, who every year dropped out of the depleting ranks of the Grand Army, and were laid to rest. The men of the newer generation, none the less patriotic, faced fresh problems and questions. They were more and more willing to bury old issues and inheritances from the four years of strife. The veterans who had faced each other through rifts of battle-smoke, or at the Bloody Angle, made up first.

I remember well being at the dinner, and present as a guest and speaker, given in Faneuil Hall, in Boston, where the Robert E. Lee Camp, of Richmond, and the John A. Andrew Post, of Boston, ate, drank, made speeches, embraced each other in friendship, "fought their battles o'er" in harmony, and pledged mutual vows of loyalty to the Union. It seemed as if, from the canvas on the walls which had reëchoed with the eloquence of Samuel Adams and Daniel Webster, the faces of the great statesmen looked down in hearty approval. Orators and poets took up the theme of reconciliation. The sectional politicians and the parsons kept up the war still longer, while those that never did any of the real fighting were last of all to yearn for and seek the benison of the Prince of Peace, " Blessed are the peacemakers."

In time the great war story was told in the bloom of art, the uprearing of monuments, the fascinations of literature and the drama, and in dispassionate narration. In the true perspective of history the men of the North and the South honor each other.

Nothing exhibits the moral stamina of the Anglo-Saxon peoples more than their capacity to accept results, when the issue has been tried and the war is over — that is, when the other side has had its innings. General Robert E. Lee set a shining example.

This war revealed also the possibilities of the men of African descent. Can their story be told better than is told on the memorial to Colonel Robert G. Shaw on Boston Common? President Eliot, of Harvard University, who has written of "American Contributions to Civilization," thus puts a stout volume in a few words: —

"The black rank and file volunteered when disaster clouded the Union cause; served without pay for eighteen months, till given that of white troops; faced threatened enslavement if captured; were brave in action, patient under heavy and dangerous labors, and cheerful amid hardships and privations.

"Together they gave to the nation and the world undying proof that Americans of African descent possess the pride, courage, and devotion of the patriot soldier. One hundred and eighty thousand such Americans enlisted under the Union flag in MDCCCLXIII–MDCCCLXV."

CHAPTER XXV.

AMERICAN MARINES AND SAILORS IN KOREA.

OUT from the mainland of China rises the mountainous island of Formosa, or the Beautiful, so named by the Portuguese who were first struck with its attractive form. Japanese navigators came here in old days, but so long ago that the history of their expeditions has become nursery and fairy tales. Only in recent centuries have Chinese settled on the shores and plains, especially in the north, and not until 1683 did they take possession and assume the government of the island.

The Formosan camphor trees are the most wonderful in the world. This is the land of the sky-blue bamboo. No island, perhaps, in all the earth is so rich in timber. In the mountains and on the east coast live the copper-colored, head-hunting aborigines. They belong to that great drift of humanity in the island world, from the Philippines to the Alaska peninsula, which extends in a circle and has furnished the ancestors of the North American Indians. The more civilized Japanese, who are also relatives to these red men, and used to cut off their enemy's heads after every battle, have, in the orderly evolution of time, changed head-hunting into a game of polo, in which red and white balls take the place of human skulls.

The American bark *Rover*, whose captain had also his family with him, was wrecked in southeastern Formosa, and all on board were murdered. As the Chinese mandarins could do nothing, Admiral Bell, on June 13, 1867, landed a force of nearly two hundred marines and sailors from the war steamers *Hartford* and *Wyoming*. Our men plunged into the bamboo jungles to punish these savages, and perhaps cannibals. In the tangled thickets it was hardly possible to see more than a few feet ahead, and the red rascals knew the ground far better than the white strangers. It was so hot and so moist, so gloomy and twilight-like, that it was like fighting a battle in a bathroom filled with steam. All that our men could do was to burn a few huts. Only occasionally did they catch sight of the flash of a gun barrel or see a puff of smoke. How many were slain on the Formosan side is not known, but one of our brave and gallant officers, Alexander Slidell MacKenzie, was killed. He was buried in the garden of the British consulate at Takao. When the funeral was over, one of the officers named Sigsbee, who was a good artist, made a sketch of the sad scene for MacKenzie's family and sent it to them. Sigsbee was afterward commander of the battleship *Maine*, destroyed in Havana harbor in 1898.

Although Korea still kept herself shut off from the world, thinking herself safe, her very isolation tempted marauders. Our American sailors shipwrecked on her shores were fed and escorted over the frontier and delivered to the United States Consul at Newchwang in Manchuria.

This was the seaport at which during the year 1894–1895 the United States steamship *Alert* was fixed for the winter, lying inside of a sort of dry dock made by excavating the mud and surrounding her by earthwork fortification. Covered over with canvas, the ship served as a fort for the protection of American interests in that region during the Chinese and Japanese war.

A German Jew, a French Catholic priest, and the renegade son of an American Protestant missionary, with a lot of the riffraff of humanity, mostly Chinese, collected from the wharves of Shanghai, with some Manila men from the Philippines, made a raid into Korea in 1866. The American supplied the money. Feron, the French priest, was pilot, and Oppert, the Hebrew, commanded the motley expedition. Running their little steamer up a certain river at high tide, they marched overland. They expected, with coal shovels, to open the grave and dig up the bones of the Korean Regent's ancestors, in order to hold them to ransom. They would thus compel him to open the country to foreign trade.

Instead of a plain grave, they found a granite mausoleum. Unable to make much impression on heavy masonry, and being pressed by the infuriated natives, they had to retreat. Thousands of angry Koreans gathered menacingly about them. Afterward, when landing on the island of Kangwa to steal sheep in order to get fresh mutton, they were fired upon, and a Manila man was wounded. This caused the Spanish Consul to begin an investigation, which brought out the facts in the case. Yet no one was convicted or imprisoned. Is it any wonder that the Koreans did not at first take kindly to intercourse with Americans?

Another expedition of illegal entrance into Korean waters, and therefore piratical, was made in this same year. Whether for lawful or unlawful purposes, is not known, for no one survived to tell the tale. In August the schooner *General Sherman* went up the Ping Yang River. The crew consisted of the owner, master, and mate, who were Americans, a Scottish missionary, who wished to learn the Korean language, and an Englishman with a Chinese money-counter, or expert, called a shroof, beside the pilot and force of Chinese working the craft. The cargo consisted of cotton cloth, glass, tin plate, and such other articles as the Koreans were likely to want. This was called "an experimental trading voyage," and may have been honestly so called. But when the *General Sherman* got into the river and near Ping Yang city, the Koreans, with fire rafts, bows and arrows, and matchlocks, attacked and killed them all and then burned up the vessel. Years afterward a brave young officer named John G. Bernadou, who in the Spanish war of 1898 commanded the *Winslow*, on which Ensign Bagley was killed and he himself wounded, went up into North Korea and investigated the affair of the *General Sherman*.

Two of our ships — the *Wachusett*, Captain Febiger, and afterward the *Ticonderoga*, Commodore Shufeldt — were despatched to Korean waters; but receiving little or no satisfaction it was thought necessary, in 1870, to send out a squadron under Commodore John Rodgers, with our minister to China on board, to make a treaty; or, if necessary, to chastise the Koreans. Soon there were assembled on the Chinese coast at Tientsin the following vessels of war: *Colorado*, Admiral Farragut's old flagship, and so handsome that it was called in the East by the French officers "*La Belle Frégate*," the corvette *Alaska*, and the smaller vessels *Ashuelot* and *Monocacy*. The latter was a double-ender, long and narrow, having a rudder at each extremity so that she could become stem or stern at will. By this time the British had begun to build ironclads, and our wooden vessels, although neat and trim, looked to the British and French officers very old-fashioned and antiquated. The Koreans, under the direction of the Regent, or Tai Wen Kun, built eight forts on the Han River, made bullet-proof cotton coats, and ironclad helmets of many thicknesses of cotton cloth, and prepared with the tiger hunters and other men used to spears, arrows, and firearms to resist the American invaders.

The squadron arrived off Boisée Island, at the mouth of the Han River, on May 30. Twelve days later, the two lighter war steamers and the steam launches, under command of Captain Blake, moved up to survey. When our men had rounded the bend where the water ran in a narrow channel a hundred yards wide, making almost a whirlpool, they saw to their surprise a new earthwork, in which scores of small cannon were as numerous as if ranged on the floor of an arsenal. Only a few thirty-two pounders had been mounted in the embrasures; but on heavy logs, nailed or lashed together in groups of five, were clumsy jingals or breech-loading cannon, like those used by Cortez and Pizarro hundreds of years before. In these, the iron breech could be taken out, filled with a cartridge, and then replaced and pinned down, losing much of the powder's force at the joint. In some of the rude guns was, not one touch-hole, but a row of vents to help the poor powder ignite more quickly.

The Korean general had expected to open on the Americans just as they turned the rocky point and sink the whole line of steam launches, after the two steamers had forged ahead. The treacherous rascal was a moment too late in giving the signal to fire. Our men were wet to the skin with the splash of the river, lashed by hundreds of missiles; but only one American was wounded, and none of the boats was hurt. The little steam launches soon opened their bow guns, and the four brass howitzers began to play. The *Palos* and *Monocacy*, somewhat ahead of the launches, turned back and soon their ten-inch shells were dropping among the white-coated Koreans, who fled from the fort, leaving it empty and silent.

Commodore Rodgers waited ten days for the Korean government, or local officers, to make apology for their treachery; but no apology came. A landing force was therefore organized to attack and destroy the whole line of forts, seven in number, and built on the bluffs fronting the river. Twenty boats and four launches were to be towed by the *Palos* and *Monocacy*. Ten companies of infantry, made up of 105 marines and 546 sailors, were to be put in command of Lieutenant Commander Winfield Scott Schley. The *Monocacy* had her battery increased with two nine-inch guns from the *Colorado*.

On the 10th of June the chastising expedition moved up the Han River. The heavy guns of the *Monocacy* first breached the stone walls and then emptied the first fort with her shells. Our men landed at a point below the fort, and went into camp, after destroying everything destructible inside the fort. The marines occupied a post in advance to guard against a rush from the Koreans, who, dressed in white, could be seen like ghosts moving about in the darkness and occasionally firing on our pickets. Under the stars our men lay down to rest before the day of toil and glory that awaited them on the morrow, which was Sunday.

The next day the reveille was sounded and the men called to breakfast. After everything combustible in the fort, including the provisions of rice and dried fish, had been piled up and set on fire, the march began at seven o'clock, with the river on the right. The rough roads were only bridle paths through rice swamps and over hills. The marines led the advance, and the sailors dragged their Dahlgren howitzers up hill and down dale. Coming to the middle line of intrenchments, the land force had only to wait while the good ship dropped her shells inside the fort, which made the white-coats fly without firing their guns. It seems curious, but such is the fact, that in the Japanese invasion of Korea in 1592 the Koreans invented and used bombshells, which they called "Heaven-shaking thunder," and even built ironclad ships or tortoise-armored men-of-war to resist the Japanese. Now they had only matchlocks and jingals.

Our men entered and tumbled the sixty brass cannon of two-inch bore over the cliffs into the river. Then under the hot sun they resumed the march in the steaming heat. The pioneers, sappers, and miners mended the road by cutting bushes, filling hollows, and widening the paths.

Meanwhile the Koreans had gathered in large masses on the left, evidently hoping to get into the rear and make an attack with a rush, while our men were getting ready to storm the main fort. To checkmate this move, a detachment of three companies with five howitzers were posted so as to guard the flank and rear of our main body. The sailors in two detachments had to be quick in getting the guns in position,— three on one hill and two on the other,— for the natives charged up the hill in the very teeth of the shells from the howitzers fired at both long and short range. Our artillerists used shrapnel, or bombs filled with bullets, which not only explode but drive each ball with a musket's force. Coolly they took aim, and their fine practice saved the day. The Koreans were driven back and scattered. Often one exploding shell seemed to make twenty men first to leap into the air and then fall dead or wounded.

The *Monocacy* out in the river moved abreast of our men, and threw bombs into the main fort on the promontory, just eastward of the rocky point, from which the Koreans had fired on our boats on June 1. The nine-inch shells pierced the walls and dropped into the forts, but the garrison bravely held their ground. The howitzers on the hilltops, now free, turned their muzzles and fired into the fort, over the heads of our men, who were resting in the cool ravine before charging up the hill. This citadel, the key to the whole line of fortifications, was 150 feet high from the bottom of the glen. With the redoubt below it mounted 143 guns. Our ship folk were to rush up the steep acclivity, which seemed more fitted for goats to climb and birds to fly over than for marines and sailors to scale.

However, the *Monocacy's* shells had breached the walls, and through these openings our marines and blue-jackets could enter. Led by their officers, they dashed up the hill. The natives, knowing that death was sure, began to chant a patriotic song. Then, after emptying their jingals and matchlocks, they leaped on the parapet. Not being able to load quickly enough, they hurled stones at the assaulting force, and even hurled dust into the eyes of the foreigners. Then with spear and sword they rushed at our officers, who were the first inside. The first American over the parapet was Lieutenant McKee, after whom one of the new torpedo boats has been named, and whose father was also killed in a breach during the Mexican war. McKee was shot and speared, but Commander Winfield Scott Schley, now admiral, rushed to support McKee, and was made a target by the same foe. The Korean who made the lunge missed his body, and the iron blade passed between chest and arm; so Schley was saved for Santiago. Immediately a carbine bullet stretched the Korean flat. There was a terrible hand-to-hand conflict inside the fort between the men in white and in blue, but the Koreans not killed outright were chased outside in droves and shot as they ran down the hill. When the smoke cleared away, 243 corpses in white garments were counted in and around the fort, and at least one hundred were drowned or floated as corpses on the river. Only twenty prisoners, all wounded, were taken alive. Two of our men were killed and ten wounded.

After forty-eight hours on shore our naval people had captured five forts, fifty flags, and nearly five hundred pieces of artillery, of which twenty-seven were heavy cannon, and the rest jingals. On Monday morning the whole force reëmbarked. The long line of boats towed by the *Monocacy* made a splendid sight. The flags — their staves tufted with pheasant feathers, and their canvas gay with bright paintings of flying serpents, winged tigers holding lightning in their claws, mountain gods riding on piebald ponies, mountains robed in thunder clouds, and other emblems of power — decorated the masts of the *Monocacy*. At half-past ten the victors rejoined their comrades at Boisée Island, the cheers of the welcoming sailors making the woodlands ring. On July 5, after a stay of thirty-five days in Korean waters, Admiral John Rodgers returned to Chifu, in China.

CHAPTER XXVI.

OUR EXPANDING EMPIRE ON THE PACIFIC.

ON the Pacific, the greatest of oceans, the Americans were, in their enterprise, far in advance of possession. Generations before they owned an acre of land on the Pacific coast, two ships from Boston — the *Columbia*, of two hundred and twenty tons, and the sloop *Washington*, of ninety tons — had reached Nootka Sound, and passed the winter there. Captain Gray explored Queen Charlotte's Sound and the Strait of San Juan de Fuca, and having collected a cargo of furs, took them to Canton. He brought back a cargo of tea to Boston, and, having rounded Capes Horn and Good Hope, his was thus the first American vessel to carry the flag around the world.

Owing to the fact that the East India Company kept out British merchants from the Pacific trade, while Russian ships were not allowed in Chinese ports, very few vessels except those floating the stars and stripes were seen in the Pacific, or at least the northern half of it. Until 1814 the direct trade between China and all North and South

America, and on both sides of the continent, was carried on by American ships.

The Russians wished to keep our ships out of their Alaskan possessions, and they claimed the land and all the coast down to the Columbia River. Had the Russians been able to carry on their commerce without our help, they would gladly have shut out our vessels; but they could not. In 1806 the question was, for a time, settled by the American ship *Juno* coming in with provisions, and saving the Russian garrison and settlers at Sitka from dying of starvation.

The American eagle found himself between the two difficulties of trying to please both the Russian bear and the British lion, for both nations claimed a large part of the western coast of North America. In 1821 the Czar Alexander issued an ukase, declaring that the water between the northwestern coast of America, from Behring Strait to Vancouver's Island, and the coast of Asia from East Cape, in Siberia, almost down to the island of Vezo, was a closed sea. In other words, the whole Pacific Ocean north of 45° 50′ belonged to Russia. The autocrat of all the Russias said: "It is therefore prohibited to all foreign vessels, not only to land on the coasts and islands belonging to Russia, as stated above, but also to approach within less than one hundred Italian miles. The transgressor's vessel is subject to confiscation, along with the whole cargo."

This was a pretty fair specimen of the kind of action likely to be expected from the autocrat who, when shown the plans of the Russian engineers for the making of a railway from Moscow to St. Petersburg, simply took a ruler and, drawing on the map a straight line between the two points, said, "Let that be the route." In spite of all the expense involved, and the difficulties in the way, this became the route. But the United States never approved of monarchy, which means one-man power.

At this time none of our people, so far as known at that time, could read Russian. Indeed, even as late as forty years ago, no English-speaking person could read a book written in Japanese or Korean. The accounts of the first explorers in the northern Pacific, being expressed in the Muscovite's tongue, and not yet translated into English, were unknown, and therefore the Czar's claims were mistrusted by our government. Mr. John Adams, after perusing all the books of travel and discovery in this region of the earth that he could get, found that the Russians' claims were not thoroughly well grounded. He wrote in his diary, "I find proof enough to put down the Russian government; but how shall we answer the Russian cannon?" When Mr. Adams met the Czar's minister, Baron de Tuyl, who was a very agreeable gentleman, he set forth very strongly what has since become the Monroe Doctrine. Perhaps this is the first clear expression of it in American history.

Mr. Adams said, "I told him specially that we should contest the right of Russia to any territorial establishment on this continent; and that we should assume distinctly the principle that the American continents are no longer subjects for any new European colonial establishment."

The Russian Baron was troubled because Commodore Hull, of *Old Ironsides* fame, was going to take command of a Pacific squadron, and some of the toasts drunk at his farewell dinner seemed to be warlike in tone. It was feared there might be bloodshed between the Americans and the Russian cruisers. Happily for both countries, two good men were at work. A liberal treaty was made, in which the autocrat gave up his tremendous claim. The boundary line of Russian America was fixed at $54°\ 40'$. Intoxicating liquors, firearms, weapons, powder, or munitions of war were forbidden to be sold to the natives. It was evident that the Russian Emperor was entering into the spirit of the age, and wished to stand well in the world's public opinion.

This dispute attracted much public attention.

The British were glad that our country had become the leading power in arresting the expansive ambition of Russia. Our own newspapers were full of lively paragraphs and squibs, which showed that the United States did not intend to submit quietly to the decrees of an autocrat.

The Baltimore *Chronicle* of May 10, 1823, published this lively bit of doggerel: —

> "Old Neptune one morning was seen on the rocks,
> Shedding tears by the pailful, and tearing his locks;
> He cried, 'a *Land Lubber* has stole, on this day,
> Full four thousand miles of my ocean away;
>
> "'He swallows the earth' (he exclaims with emotion),
> 'And then to quench appetite, *slap* goes the ocean;
> Brother Jove must look out for his skies, let me tell ye,
> Or the Russian will bury them all in his belly.'"

This treaty and the succeeding discussions at St. Petersburg deepened the old friendship between America and Russia. This had begun as far back as the time when William Penn and Czar Peter enjoyed a friendly talk on disarmament and the federation of nations. It was increased by the action of Queen Catherine, who would hire no Russian mercenaries to help George III in his attempted subjugation of Americans. It was continued when, in 1813, Dashkoff, the Russian minister at Washington, offered, by direction of the Czar, that friendly mediation which issued in the Treaty of Ghent. Commodore M. C. Perry visited Cronstadt in the United States ship *Concord*, taking John Randolph, our minister, there, and this time we had at least one American, Professor Jenks, who could talk Russian.

Later on, Americans helped to build the Russian railways, even as they are doing now. When proud nobles, who looked down upon these gentlemen from Philadelphia, who had been educated, as Washington had been, to be engineers, the white Czar, in the brilliant ball-room and before all the dignitaries of the empire, honored them by walking arm in arm with his guests from beyond the sea. After this our countrymen were honored by all.

The two peoples became better acquainted with each other, and commerce increased. There was mutual sympathy when the Czar set free the serfs and President Lincoln emancipated the negro slaves. Again responsive chords were struck, when both liberators met death at the hands of the assassin, — one by the pistol of a fanatic and the other by the dynamite glass-bomb of an anarchist. During our Civil War, had Great Britain begun hostilities against us, a Russian fleet was ready in waiting in our waters to lend us assistance, and the Russians would have been our allies.

The charter of the Russian-American company, which had a monopoly of the fur trade, was renewed in 1839. From this date until 1859 British and American vessels were not allowed to trade in the ports of Russian America, and difficulties arose. Eight years later, all questions were settled by the treaty negotiated by Mr. Seward, and ratified by the Senate in special session March 30, 1867. For the sum of $7,200,000, all the Russian possessions in America were sold outright, without any incumbrance, and became part of the United States.

Mr. Seward was a far-sighted patriot and one of the ablest in the long line of American diplomatists. Like Washington, Jefferson, Jackson, Cass, Marcy, and other great statesmen of either party, Seward was a firm believer in the right and duty of national expansion. In his speech at Sitka, in 1869, he prophesied that, —

"The Pacific Ocean, its shores, its islands, and the vast region beyond will become the chief theatre of events in the world's great hereafter."

In 1852, in his eulogy of Henry Clay, he had said : —

"We are rising to another and more sublime stage of national progress — that of expanding wealth and rapid territorial aggrandizement.

"Our institutions throw a broad shadow across the St. Lawrence, and, stretching beyond the valley of Mexico, reach even to the plains of Central America; while the Sandwich Islands and the shores of China recognize their renovating influence. Wherever that influence is felt, a desire for protection under those institutions is awakened.

"Expansion seems to be regulated, not by any difficulties of resistance, but by the moderation which results from our own internal constitution. No one knows how rapidly that restraint may give way. Who can tell how far or how fast it ought to yield? Commerce has brought the ancient continents near to us, and created necessities for new positions, — perhaps connections or colonies there, — and with the trade and friendship of the elder nations, their conflicts and collisions are brought to our doors and to our hearts. Our sympathy kindles, or indifference extinguishes, the fires of freedom in foreign lands. Before we shall be fully conscious that a change is going on in Europe, we may find ourselves once more divided by that eternal line of separation that leaves on the one side those of our citizens who obey the impulses of sympathy, while on the other are found those who submit only to the counsels of prudence. Even prudence will soon be required to decide whether distant regions, east and west, shall come under our own protection, or be left to aggrandize a rapidly spreading domain of hostile despotism."

Out in the Pacific Ocean, nearly midway between America and Asia, though nearer to the United

States, is a group of twelve islands. They form an archipelago, containing a land area of about seven thousand square miles, or nearly as large as New Jersey. These islands have a lovely climate and fertile soil, and are rich in minerals. The whole group is volcanic, and some of them with the largest craters in the world are here still active. Beside forests and much timber, there are about two million acres of grazing land and two hundred and ninety thousand acres of arable soil, with plenty of streams flowing down from the mountains to the sea. The chief object of culture is the sugar-cane. On forty or fifty plantations about forty thousand tons of sugar are produced annually. Many other rich products are exported. Of the $35,000,000 at which the sugar plantations were valued, about $25,000,000 were owned by Americans.

The Hawaiian Islands were first discovered by a Spanish navigator in 1542. Captain Cook, the English explorer, made them better known by his visit in 1778, and by his death there in 1779. There had been long series of wars; but the people had emerged from barbarism and a feudal system was in operation. In 1790 Kamehameha defeated another chief or king, and after several years of hard fighting became master of the archipelago. He was greatly assisted to get arms and supplies by the wealth which he gained in selling sandalwood to the American and Chinese merchants. By and by came a struggle between the progressives, who wished to overthrow the taboo system, which put so much power in the hands of the pagan priests, and those who held to old ways. After a bloody battle, lasting six hours, the conservatives were overthrown. Then began the universal destruction of idols. When in 1820 the first missionaries, fourteen in number, — seven men with their wives, — arrived from the United States, the modern history of Hawaii began. The language was reduced to writing, and printing flourished. In 1825 the Ten Commandments were adopted as the basis of the national laws. In 1840, Kamehameha III and the chiefs formed a constitution which gave civil rights to the people.

Our first treaty was made with the Hawaiian government through Captain Catesby Ap Jones. Several attempts were made by British and French to seize the islands and hold them, but they were not permanently successful. Meanwhile American interests were increasing. Usually the native government was carried on intelligently and peacefully, though there was a riot in 1874, which was put down by armed forces from the British and the United States war vessels lying at Honolulu. In 1887 a progressive party demanded a new constitution, which King Kalakaua accepted. Soon after this the king and queen and Liliuokalani visited Boston, where I had the pleasure of meeting and talking with both. When the king died, Liliuokalani succeeded to the throne as queen. She was thoroughly opposed to the new constitution. When after she had defied the will of the legislature in favor of the opium and baser interests, it was believed that she intended to proclaim a new constitution, restoring the royal power, a small but influential portion of the citizens rose against her and formed a provisional government.

Our American minister at this time was the Hon. John L. Stevens. He was a pure patriot, a man of ability, and long diplomatic experience in South America and Scandinavia, and one of those accomplished envoys who have done our country honor abroad. He knew the situation well. He felt sure that if the baser element had any opportunity, they would destroy foreign property and begin incendiarism. From the United States man-of-war *Boston*, then lying in the harbor at Honolulu, he ordered a party of marines and sailors to be landed for the protection of American life and property.

The provisional government at once took steps to secure the favor of the United States. Each party, of the deposed queen and of the government, sent representatives to Washington. President Harrison warmly approved of the idea of annexation. A treaty making Hawaii part of the United States was sent to the Senate for ratification. For this the new Hawaiian government petitioned; but we had then no national policy on the subject. When President Cleveland came into power he withdrew the treaty, disapproved of the action of Mr. Stevens, and sent a "paramount" agent to Honolulu to secure neutrality. Nevertheless, on July 4, 1894, the republic of Hawaii was proclaimed, and Sanford B. Dole became President. With wisdom and ability the Hawaiian republic was governed, until, in 1898, it became an integral part of the United States. Then the action of John L. Stevens was vindicated.

CHAPTER XXVII.

OUR WAR WITH SPAIN.

FOR centuries the people living on the seacoast lands of western Europe imagined that there was somewhere, out in the Atlantic Ocean, a group of islands which must be passed before the continent, still further on, could be reached. The notion existed that during the invasion of the Moors, some Christian bishops and their flocks had fled to these islands and there found peace and prosperity. Gradually the legend took the form of islands exquisitely beautiful, and endlessly rich in gold, silver, pearls, and gems. These were the anti-insulæ or Antilles, that is, the islands before you came to the continent.

In 1492 Columbus discovered Cuba and other West India Islands, and later the American continent was made known. So then, here were the Antilles — a name applied to all the islands in the Gulf and adjacent waters except the Bahamas. The Greater Antilles are Cuba, Hayti, Jamaica, and Porto Rico, with the islets clustered near them. The Lesser Antilles, or Windward Islands, form a crescent, with the convex side toward the east.

As Cuba was the first, so has it always been the chief colony of Spain. It was born into the world through volcanic action, and the Copper Mountains traverse its whole length, the highest summit being about 7750 feet high. Cuba is rich in almost everything that can satisfy the wants of man, and by which he can make money, such as sugar, molasses, rum, tobacco, coffee, fruit, wax, copper, metals, and minerals, the useful and precious woods, with almost every sort of food, and pastures for great herds of cattle.

Although the rivers are all small and not navigable, there are good harbors, with deep water, at Havana, Matanzas, Puerto Principe, Santiago de Cuba, and other places. Under good government this island ought to be the pearl of all on earth; yet its history is one of human wretchedness. One contrasts it at once with another typical island, Java, of same size and with a similar climate, but Java has a much larger and happier population and vastly more wealth, while the government of its eleven millions is so good that little is heard of it. Java is happy to have had no history like that of Cuba.

The first Spaniards who colonized Cuba, in 1511, treated the natives so cruelly that in forty-two years the Indian population had become extinct. Cuba was the centre of the slave trade in Spanish America, and during the height of its activity, from 1789 to 1845, five hundred and fifty thousand slaves were brought into the island. The negroes rose up against their masters in 1844–1848, but their uprisings were put down with awful slaughter, about ten thousand suffering death in 1848. The whole story of the island is one of turmoil and bad government.

It was thought, even early in this century, that the United States must possess Cuba for the sake of self-defence. Our commerce was disturbed by misrule and periodical anarchy. Havana was the hotbed of yellow fever, which desolated our cities. The utter lack of drainage and sanitary system, with the accumulated filth in the Spanish towns, formed the soil for the growth of pestilence from which our country suffered. The vultures, nature's scavengers and living crucibles, abound in Spanish-American towns.

During President Polk's administration a strong pressure was put upon our government, mainly from the South, to obtain "the Pearl of the Antilles." A hundred millions of dollars were offered for Cuba in 1848, but refused. In the insurrections which followed, the influence of American adventurers was noticeable. When the revolution broke out in Spain, in 1868, the Cubans tried again to win their independence. War began, which lasted twelve years. During this time, in 1873, the steamer *Virginius*, with about fifty Americans on board to assist the Cuban insurgents, led by General Cespedes, was captured by the Spanish man-of-war *Tornado*. All of the volunteers were put to death, under circumstances of such wanton cruelty that the moral sense of the American people was outraged, and it was felt that nothing similar would ever be allowed again. The losses and devastations on both sides were awful; but in 1880 the hopes of the patriots were blasted, for the Spaniards had crushed the uprising. Yet the island was left in disorder, and the public debt amounted to $85,000,000.

In 1895 a new insurrection broke out, and the Cuban republic was organized. Its flag, of blue and white stripes, had a white star set on a red triangular ground.

To put down this fresh uprising, and that in the Philippines which soon followed, Spain put forth all her resources, poured corps after corps, even to her full military strength, into the island. She sent her very best soldiers, and tens of thousands of her ablest young men, until her army in Cuba numbered over a hundred thousand. The patriots could gather only a few hundred men at a time for skirmishes, ambuscades, dashing raids, or cavalry charges on detached bodies of the enemy. Yet the Spaniards died by the thousands. While bullets and the machete killed hundreds, disease carried off tens of thousands. When Marshal Campos was recalled for lack of energy, General Weyler, who had been in the Philippines, was sent to Cuba. He was a soldier of the type of the Duke of Alva. He began war in an uncivilized and mediæval way. Indeed, he reminded one of an Assyrian conqueror and the unspeakable brutality of war in early ages. His policy was to slaughter and burn wherever his soldiers could go. He compelled the pacificos, or quiet people of the disturbed districts, to leave their homes and farms and to be reconcentrated upon reservations. There, without food or means of support, they died of disease and starvation by the tens of thousands.

Meanwhile, with our Cuban commerce ruined and the sufferings of the reconcentrados exciting sympathy and indignation throughout the United States, our government put pressure upon Spain to recognize the independence of Cuba. It had come to be a very costly matter for our government to keep watch, to prevent relief ships from sailing for Cuba, and to maintain neutrality, when so many thousands of our young men wanted to help the insurgents. The Spanish government recalled Weyler and sent Marshal Blanco. For a while a profession was made of giving the Cubans something like self-government.

Meanwhile the insurgents of the Philippine Islands were making progress against their oppressors. Even the Spanish army of twenty thousand men sent there could make little headway. Not knowing what complications might ensue in the Far East, our government reënforced the Asiatic squadron. Our old wooden vessels, except the historic *Monocacy*, had been brought home. A fine new fleet of modern steel ships floated the American flag in the Pacific. On the 3d of January, 1898, Commodore George Dewey hoisted his pennant on board the flagship *Olympia*.

When the wonderful year of 1898, so crowded with decisive and significant events all over the world, dawned, it showed that the Spaniards in Havana were resenting the American indignation against Spanish cruelties. The lives of Americans, and even of Consul General Lee (son of the great Confederate general), were threatened. The United States notified Spain that a ship of war, the *Maine*, would be sent on a friendly visit to Cuba. A reciprocal courtesy was shown by the despatch of the Spanish armored cruiser *Viscaya* to the harbor of New York. During this vessel's stay in our waters, extraordinary precautions were taken by our national, state, and municipal authorities to prevent any injury or hostile action by irresponsible persons. Meanwhile the American public opinion was still further inflamed by two episodes. One was the exposure of a letter to a friend from the Spanish minister at Washington, in which he abused and slandered President McKinley. The other was a request from the Spanish government for the recall of Consul General Lee, which was refused.

While all the elements of a volcanic explosion of public feeling were thus at hand, telegrams from Havana, on the night of February 15, 1898, sent a wave of horror and indignation over the country. It was like a great oceanic movement, almost certain to overwhelm all barriers and force war. The *Maine* was a second-class battle-ship in command of Captain Sigsbee. On arriving, she was led and placed at her anchorage by Spanish officers of the port. About nine o'clock in the evening a terrible submarine eruption turned a magnificent ship into a mass of scrap metal, and blew 259 of her officers and crew into eternity. For four weeks the people waited for the verdict from the board of inquiry. A unanimous decision was reached on March 21, that the ship was destroyed by the explosion of a submarine mine, or, in other words, as the people interpreted, by Spanish treachery.

By this time the war fever had reached the boiling point. As our harbors were practically defenceless, Congress voted unanimously $50,000,000 for national defence. Immediately there began in the War and Navy Departments tremendous activity. Competent agents were sent to Europe, and materials and ships were bought at home and abroad. Our harbors were mined, and most of the lights on the coast were extinguished. Property at watering places depreciated, and thousands of Americans, who had expected to spend their summer vacation in Europe, changed their plans. Every one saw that war was coming, and that this time our government would not allow the old state of things in Cuba to go on. President McKinley endeavored to avert war and advised the non-recognition of the so-called Cuban republic. General Lee remained in Havana till April 10, bravely superintending the removal of the American refugees.

On the 18th of April, by joint resolution of Congress, war was declared, the President signing the document April 20. Yet our minister at Madrid, General Stuart L. Woodford, was not allowed to present the American ultimatum to Spain, for at seven o'clock on the morning of April 21 he received his passports from the Spanish minister. This constituted the actual beginning of war.

President McKinley proclaimed the blockade of the coast of Cuba on April 21, and two days later issued a call for one hundred and twenty-five thousand volunteers. The regular army was concentrated at Chickamauga, and soon our brave veterans were "tenting on the old camp ground," amid the inspiring scenery and memories of the great battle in which General Thomas had won his title of "the Rock." At Tampa, a bustling city in Florida, where, over three centuries ago, the Spaniards landed with bloodhounds and manacles for enslaving the Indians, a great camp was laid out for the concentration and acclimatizing of our troops.

Now, for the first time in American history, the United States, by act of the chief executive, gave up privateering as a relic of barbarism. In a clear and strong state paper President McKinley adhered to the Declaration of Paris, while Congress passed a bill to provide war revenue. Soon the stamps on bank checks, express receipts, business documents, telegrams, and various articles bought and sold, reminded one of the war days of 1861. Business went on as usual. Indeed, during this year, 1898, the volume of traffic, domestic and foreign, done, exceeded that of any year previously known; yet the expenditures of the government were very great.

CHAPTER XXVIII.

THE AMERICAN FLAG IN THE PHILIPPINES.

AGAIN, in 1898, as always in our history before, it was to be demonstrated that, opportunity given, the navy excels the army, for the one good reason that the navy consists of a body of trained professional men, who know their duties thoroughly, and is free from the withering influences of sectional and party politics. It is an ever efficient national arm of defence. On the other hand, in a great war, regular and amateur soldiers are mixed together, and the true army, unlike the navy, is not allowed to show what it can do by itself. The organization of the volunteer forces is honeycombed with favoritism, partisan politics, and a thousand other influences which destroy the efficiency of a noble body of men, whose energies are wasted, and whose aims are often defeated, by moral diseases from which the navy is free.

The navy was instantly ready and efficient. Of the four officers called to lead and strike at once, I had the pleasure of knowing three, their records and abilities and personal qualities. Having also a somewhat close acquaintance with the history and status of the navy, by examination of the records and acquaintance with the ships, I had no anxiety, from the first, for this branch of the service. I knew Captain Sampson as an expert in the theory and practice of modern naval artillery. He had long been in chief charge of the practice grounds at Indian Head. In the Naval Observatory at Washington, where I first met him among the chronometers, micronometers, and all the delicate instruments for measuring time and space, he struck me as one of the most accomplished men I had ever seen. Not because his ordinary rank would entitle him, but because of his consummate abilities, and to the great delight of the whole navy, he was chosen to command the fleet, which sailed April 22 from Key West to begin the blockade of the Cuban ports.

Commodore Winfield Scott Schley was given command of the Flying Squadron, which made rendezvous at Hampton Roads in Chesapeake Bay. I had known him in Japan, and of his shining record in the Korean war, where he led the land expedition which destroyed the Han forts in 1871. Bold, alert, and dashing, Schley waited for Admiral Cervera, who, with the armored cruisers *Viscaya*, *Oquendo*, *Christobal Colon*, *Maria Teresa*, and three torpedo-boat destroyers, made rendezvous at the Cape Verde Islands. For many days the whole American coast was in suspense. All asked "Whence? whither?"

when?" but none could answer. Our swift cruisers, one of the best being the *Cincinnati* under Captain Chester, and many fast despatch boats, patrolled the coast from Eastport to Point Isabel. Yet nothing was heard of Cervera until he appeared off Martinique in the West Indies.

It was wisely thought best to be thoroughly prepared for the whole Spanish fleet, and so word had been early sent to the captain of the battle-ship *Oregon* on the Pacific coast to come eastward. To make this journey round Cape Horn, would be a superb test of the quality, speed, and efficiency of American-built battle-ships. For years we had heard criticisms and objections about the foolishness of building a navy of the modern type. The objectors supposed that we had neither the workmen to plan and build, nor men to man and control modern battle-ships, and that such enterprise must be left to Great Britain because of her longer naval history, and whose admirals and sailors had more naval experience. These were not the objections of Europeans, but of Americans. It was somewhat different from the idea of the young lady who, visiting a modern British man-of-war when the stars and stripes floated over wooden ships only, was told by the captain that in another war between Great Britain and the United States the former would surely win. Her only reply was "What, again?"

In sixty-eight days, at every moment ready for the enemy, the *Oregon* made her journey of fourteen thousand miles from Puget Sound to Key West, arriving without a screw loose or a bolt started, at Key West.

Captain J. C. Watson was another officer who, when younger, had, like Schley, served under Farragut. I had known him in the waters of Japan, where he was in command of the *Idaho* at Yokohama. To me he impersonated the idea of discipline — whether against unjust superiors, mutinous crews or deserters, or fascinating ladies and gentlemen who for fun or pleasure would have relaxed the rules which are the very soul of the service.

Another young officer, with whose record and abilities I was well acquainted, was Captain John Bernadou, who had shown great courage and coolness in Korea.

While anxiety as to the whereabouts of Cervera's fleet was exercising the minds of our people, exciting news came by way of Spain from the other end of the earth. It was that Commodore Dewey had attacked the fleet under Admiral Montojo, and after sinking some ships had ceased operations to land his wounded. During several days of suspense, it was uncertain as to how far successful he had been.

Soon the full story came in. The nation was thrilled with delight. Smiles broke out on every face.

During a month or so, puns upon the Commodore's name were wrought, with various degrees of wit and vileness. Congress gave him thanks, made him an Admiral, and voted him a sword.

On receiving orders to seek out and destroy the Spanish fleet, Admiral Dewey proceeded to Cavité Bay. At 5.41 A.M., on May 1, the word from the Commodore was, "You may fire when you are ready, Captain Gridley." At once the battle began. Our ships made five courses, sinking or setting fire to three Spanish ships. At 7.35, Dewey's supply of ammunition having been heavily drawn on, and the effect of our fire on the Spaniards being uncertain, "the crews left their guns and went to breakfast." When this meal was over, the signal "close for action" was hoisted, and the work of destruction was continued, the whole Spanish fleet of fourteen war vessels being sunk or destroyed. Not a man on the American side was killed, and but seven were wounded. It was, what in ancient times would have been called, a miracle.

This victory was the beginning of American expansion and possessions in the Pacific, and of successful diplomacy with the Turks. Major-General Wesley Merritt was sent out with an army of about twelve thousand men. Under Generals Anderson and Greene, and with the aid of the insurgents, they invested the city of Manila. During the withdrawal of Aguinaldo and his men, to celebrate some festival on the night of July 31, the Spaniards made an attack upon our lines, and for a while demoralized the volunteers, until the regulars came to their aid and drove the Spaniards back. At noon, on the afternoon of August 18, after an attack by sea and land, the city capitulated. Soon after this the American force in Luzon numbered twenty thousand men.

The Philippines are the gateway to China, and open the door to an enormous trade and a permanent market. On the way out from San Francisco, our officers took possession of the Ladrone Islands and hoisted the American flag. On the 7th of July, 1898, Congress, by joint resolution, annexed the republic of Hawaii. The ceremony was simply but impressively accomplished on the 12th of August. The action of our minister, John L. Stevens, in 1891, in raising the American flag and landing the marines at Honolulu, from the man-of-war *Boston*, to protect American life and property, was thus vindicated. A commission of five statesmen was appointed to recommend to Congress such legislation concerning the Hawaiian Islands as they should deem necessary and proper.

CHAPTER XXIX.

SANTIAGO AND PORTO RICO.

TO return to the Atlantic, Cervera compelled by need of water and provisions entered "without incident," as his telegram told, the harbor of Santiago at the eastern end of Cuba, where a long stretch of coast had been left unblockaded. The two squadrons of Schley and Sampson now united off the entrance, and Cervera was "bottled up." Yet our navy could not follow into the harbor on account of submarine mines. Bombardment without much effect was made upon the forts on May 31, showing clearly that a land force would be necessary to take the city. The neck of Santiago harbor being like that of a bottle, a design was formed not only to put in a cork, but to wire it fast, so that the Spanish squadron could not get out. As storms might disperse our fleet and give Cervera an opportunity to slip out, Constructor R. P. Hobson with seven men volunteered to take in by night the steam collier *Merrimac*, and sink her in the narrowest part of the channel and thus block it. In the face of the fire from the Spanish batteries, this was done on the night of June 3. Yet after all the enterprise was a moral, but not a material, success, for a well-aimed shot struck the rudder of the *Merrimac*, rendering it helpless. When the hulk was scuttled and sunk, there was room for the whole fleet to pass when Cervera should think best. Hobson and his men, captured or rescued, were kindly treated by the Spaniards.

The commander of the army of fifteen thousand troops sent from Tampa to Santiago was Major-General W. R. Shafter. This officer having won a brilliant record during the Civil War, had also made a grand success of the army schools for the education of enlisted men. When it was objected that negroes would not, and could not, make good soldiers because they were illiterate, Shafter introduced schoolmasters. In four months, by constant drill and discipline, he had made his regiment of black men the crack organization of the army. Later he had the reputation of having a regiment fully up to the German standard of efficiency.

A century and a half ago, the British army under Admiral Vernon landed at Guantanamo in Cuba. In this expedition Lawrence Washington and Jacob van Braam, the one the elder brother and the other the military instructor of George Washington, served with the Virginia militia. In 1898 our marines landed here and held the town and adjacent country. The Spanish sharpshooters approached the post, while most of our men were enjoying a sea-bath.

They had smokeless powder, and were covered with leaves and greenery, so that they could not be easily detected. Indeed, our marines who rushed to their guns had hard work to know what to shoot at. Throughout the war our men were at constant disadvantage, because they had only the old-fashioned black or brown powder, while that used in the Mauser rifle cartridges of the Spaniards made no smoke. It was often, very often, difficult on our side to find where the enemy was. In this affair Dr. Gibbs, the first officer lost in the war, was killed.

On June 22 the army was disembarked at Daiquiri, and by sunset of the next day, or rather the 24th, the troops were all ashore. Our men began immediately marching forward. When our allies, "the army of the Cuban republic," appeared, there were detachments of tens, which, when all assembled, amounted to hundreds rather than thousands.

On the road to Santiago, about three miles from Siboney, was a strong position called Las Guasimas, where the Spaniards lay waiting for the Americans. Young's brigade and the dismounted volunteer cavalry, called the "Rough Riders," expecting no enemy near, were taken by surprise, and at first thrown into some disorder. Quickly recovering, they boldly charged and drove the enemy out of their position. Then our troops moved forward to attack the village of El Caney, but before this the hills and San Juan hills and blockhouses were to be carried. Sixteen light field-pieces, with infantry to support them, were sent forward.

At six o'clock, on the morning of July 1, the battle opened and soon became general. Though the Spaniards fought bravely and with obstinacy, they could not stand against the energy of our regulars. To complete their formation for a charge up the hill at San Juan, our men had to endure a very destructive fire. Then, after going a short distance, they found a great tangle-work made of barbed iron wire. Yet despite all obstacles, they drove the enemy from their position and held what they gained.

As the Spanish general Tando was advancing with reënforcements of eight thousand men, it was necessary to continue the struggle next day and gain a decisive victory before the Spanish forces could be strengthened. On the morning of July 2 the Spaniards began by a fierce assault, but while our forces under Kent and Wheeler drove back assaulting forces, General Lawton gained a commanding position on the right, making victory the following day nearly certain. The fighting was renewed July 3, but the enemy soon gave way and the firing ceased. Our men had lost 230 killed and 1284 wounded in the three days' fighting, and 79 were missing. The Spaniards had lost 1500 men killed and wounded.

As early as half-past eight General Shafter sent a flag of truce. He demanded of the Spanish commander the surrender of his army and of the city of Santiago. This was not acceded to, and yet there was evidence of a willingness to negotiate; for while reënforcements for our army were on their way, the Spaniards had little hope of being reënforced. Furthermore, they had lost their fleet. On Sunday morning, July 3, Admiral Cervera, under orders from Captain-General Blanco, knowing also that he would lose his ships when the city surrendered, and that while the channel was open he had a chance of success, moved out with his squadron of four Spanish armored cruisers and two torpedo boats, in single column. He then turned to the right, hoping, possibly, to destroy the United States steamship *Brooklyn*, and to save some of his fleet.

The Americans were not caught napping. Everything had been arranged and foreseen by Sampson, and Schley was ready. Signalling to all the ships to close and pursue, the most terrific naval cannonade known in modern time opened upon the Spanish ships. Within two hours after the opening gun seven thousand shot, weighing one thousand tons, had been fired, every Spanish ship was sunk, and six hundred men were killed or drowned, and nearly two thousand captured. On our side only one man was killed, and one wounded. This splendid triumph of the American navy practically ended the war. On July 17 the city and province of Santiago de Cuba, with over twenty-two thousand soldiers, was surrendered.

It was the splendid qualities of the American private soldiers, especially of the regulars, that won at Santiago. It was the superb discipline and invincible power of the navy that destroyed the two Spanish fleets in the East and the West Indies.

A very foolish controversy broke out in the newspapers concerning the relative merits, and the amount of praise and credit, due to Commodores Sampson and Schley, in the naval triumph at Santiago. To tell the simple truth, both did their duty fully and nobly. In answer to words of congratulation from an old friend, Commodore Schley, as modest as gallant, wrote the following: —

"FLAGSHIP BROOKLYN, Guantanamo Bay, Cuba.
July 31, 1898.

"MY DEAR SIR: — Thanks for your kind letter; I do not think that I deserve so much as has been said in my praise for the victory of July 3; I share its honors only with my brave comrades, and I have not forgotten that there is a God of battles, for he was surely on our side that day, blessed be his Holy Name!

Thanking you again for thinking of me, I am,
Very sincerely yours,
W. S. SCHLEY.

REV. WM. ELLIOT GRIFFIS, Ithaca, N.Y."

Porto Rico was easily taken through the military science and fine art of General Miles. The Spaniards expected that the Americans would land near San Juan, but the General directed the navy to shell the town of Ponce, while other war-ships were active near San Juan. On July 25 he disembarked his troops at Guanica near Ponce. In several spirited engagements the Spaniards were driven back with slight loss on our side. Already the larger part of the island was under our control and certain to be wholly taken, when the decisive combat, for which all preparations were made, should take place, when news arrived that the protocol of peace had been signed and hostilities were immediately suspended.

Admiral Camara had sailed from Cadiz June 15, and passed through the Suez Canal with the supposed idea of going to Manila. As this move left the coast of Spain exposed, the Eastern Squadron, under Commander J. C. Watson, was got in readiness to make a descent upon Spanish Europe in order to hasten peace. However, on July 26, the French ambassador in Washington, acting for the government at Madrid, made proposals to President McKinley for peace. The terms of our government being accepted, on August 9, the protocol was made and signed August 12. The peace commission met in Paris, October 1, and the treaty of peace was signed December 10.

Our country paid the expenses of repatriating the remnants of the Spanish army, out of which about eighty thousand had died in Cuba, mainly through disease. The evacuation proceeded during December, while in the Spanish cities held by our troops the work of civil government and reform, especially the cleaning of streets, the removal of dirt and filth, and the beginning of sanitary reform, proceeded. On the 1st of January, 1899, the American flag was hoisted over the public buildings in Havana, and Spanish rule in America, after four centuries of blight, was over.

Porto Rico was definitely ceded to the United States. It was completely evacuated by October 17. The next day the flag of the United States rose in the air over the public buildings at San Juan. Our letters were henceforward directed to Porto Rico, U. S. A. October 18 is a red-letter day in the story of American expansion. On that date, in 1867, Russia formally transferred Alaska to our flag. In 1804, on October 18, the Senate took up in executive session the treaty with France that added 1,200,000 square miles to our national domain.

CHAPTER XXX.

THE GREATER UNITED STATES.

WE pen the conclusion of our story of American Expansion on this day, April 12, 1899, when, war with Spain ended, the treaty documents duly attested and exchanged, and the President's proclamation of peace issued, relations of friendship are resumed.

Our countrymen have begun in earnest to grapple with their responsibilities in the West Indies. In Porto Rico, which is about half as large as New Jersey and one of the most thickly populated regions in the world, having nearly one million inhabitants, special attention has been given to the reform of popular education. The pioneers of our commercial, benevolent, and missionary societies are upon the ground. In point of privilege, and probably in general intelligence, the people of Porto Rico may soon be on a level with the average in the United States.

In Cuba the transfer of authority was made January 1, 1899. The difference between the American and the Spanish régime is strikingly manifest in government, sanitation, the general order that prevails, and the revival of business, though years will be required for removing the scars of war and the building up of the waste places. Beside our army of occupation, the police force of the cities has been reorganized on American models. The policy of the United States government is to employ as many as possible of the natives of the island of Cuba, and to so develop the island's resources and renovate the whole life of the people that the sincere purpose of our nation in delivering Cuba from her oppressors may be manifest to the world.

Beside Cuba and Porto Rico, the former coming under our control and the latter under our ownership by treaty, a number of smaller islands, reefs, and keys in the West Indies are under the American flag and are bonded, that is, their ownership is declared in the United States Treasury.

We turn now to the East. Surprised and electrified by the news of Dewey's victory over the Spanish fleet, our government despatched twenty thousand men to capture Manila and occupy the island of Luzon. To this work the stalwart sons of the Northwest were especially called. San Francisco was made the rendezvous, and on May 13 the first regiment of volunteers, the 2d Oregon, arrived. General Wesley Merritt, born in New York City in 1836, and a veteran of the Civil War and in

Indian campaigns, was put in command of the department of the Pacific. Before July 27, when he sailed with his staff, three expeditions had been despatched under Generals Anderson, Green, and McArthur, making in all about eleven thousand men, all of whom took part in the operations about Manila. The fourth expedition arrived after the city had fallen.

The military situation with three sets of combatants was peculiar. The Spanish lines completely encircled the city and covered all avenues of approach. Enclosing Manila and the Spanish forces again was the Filipino insurgent army of about twelve thousand men. Aguinaldo had proclaimed himself president of the Philippine Republic, had pressed the Spaniards back toward Manila, and had taken many thousands of Spanish prisoners, including four thousand men and officers. When, however, Aguinaldo, who had been profuse in his promises of assistance to the Americans against the Spaniards, protested against the landing of our soldiers in places conquered or occupied by the insurgents, all correspondence ended, for our government did not wish to recognize the insurgents as allies or bind themselves by any promises.

In the night attack of July 21, that which usually happens during a battle in darkness took place. An enormous amount of ammunition was fired off without much result and with unnecessary bloodshed. On the American side ten men were killed and thirty-three wounded, and sixty thousand shots expended. On the other side about one hundred and twenty thousand Mauser cartridges were used up.

On August 7 General Merritt and Admiral Dewey gave notice of an attack, and asked that all non-combatants be removed from the city. The surrender having been called for, the assault began on the 13th. The troops of Green and McArthur turned the Spanish line of intrenchments and moved toward the walled city. Then a flag of truce showed willingness to surrender. In taking possession, our men had a double duty to perform. It was to garrison Manila and at the same time to keep out the insurgents, thus protecting the Spanish people and their property from loot or vengeance. This duty they did well, for all outrages were prevented.

By March, 1899, the United States forces numbered over twenty thousand men, most of whom were volunteers. Almost all of these, except the 10th Pennsylvania, a Tennessee and a Kansas regiment, are northwestern men, mostly from California, Oregon, and Minnesota, and declared by General Merritt to be "of the finest material to be found anywhere in America." There was little difference between regulars and volunteers, for the former were for the most part new troops, but the officers of both were not only instructed but experienced. The health of both soldiers and sailors has been excellent. " In the navy they have the advantage of living indoors and carrying their houses with them," so that sick men on the ships were almost as scarce as killed or wounded; but the army was more exposed, the men on the picket line in the rice fields being often up to their middles in water. Provisions were good, and our men were well supplied. They took advantage of the presence of the bamboo, which is a grass or cane endlessly useful. With this they made cots or bedsteads raised above the ground, by which they escaped much discomfort and sickness.

The Americans observed great deliberation before making any display in force, for it was hoped that Aguinaldo's army would disperse and the Filipinos submit to American rule; but the ambition of Aguinaldo and his colleagues, who were mostly of good Filipino families, made peace impossible. They not only controlled the island of Luzon, but they sent detachments of their men into the other islands and compelled them to acknowledge the authority of the so-called Filipino republic. In that way they fomented opposition to the arms and government of the United States.

Thirsting for vengeance upon the Spaniards and anxious for plunder, they made a treacherous attack

upon the United States troops, hoping to capture
Manila, wreak their vengeance in bloodshed, and to
appropriate the property of those who had suppressed
them so long. Matters soon became strained. When
hostilities were opened, the Filipinos were driven
back, and our men, under General Elwell Otis, began an advance which marked the beginning of a
long series of victories. These will make a score
or more of places, hitherto unknown to Americans,
familiar on battle flags and in history.

One special blessing to Manila is found in the
waterworks, which were the provision of a private
benefactor and not of the Spanish colonial government. During the operations between February 5
and 15 these were secured, thus securing an abun-
dant water supply for the dry season. One after
another the positions of the Filipinos were forced,
until by the middle of April our army had occupied
the region around Manila, including the line of railway, and had gained several advantageous points
on several islands in the archipelago, such as Iloilo
and other port cities, where trade has already begun.
The typical method of American occupation was
shown in the capture of Santa Cruz by General
Lawton. He established his headquarters at the
palace, a guard was at once placed in the church, and
within an hour the city was thoroughly patrolled,
to prevent looting. In every place entered by our

troops the natives were made to see that the American flag always means law, order, and opportunity for improvement.

Meanwhile, as fresh reënforcements are sent forward, there is presented beside the arrows of war the olive branch of peace, for the American eagle carries both. President McKinley had appointed and sent out in due season a commission headed by Jacob Gould Schurman, president of Cornell University. In a document of great clearness and simplicity, which was translated into Spanish and Tagal, the Filipinos were assured of the good purpose of the United States government to possess the whole archipelago, to heal the ravages of war, and to begin at once reform of abuses and the foundation of a new civilization in which peace, education, and opportunity for each man to enjoy fully the fruits of his labor should be within the reach of all.

The facts that many of the regular troops in our country wished to join the regiments ordered to Luzon, and that not a few of the volunteers have signified their intention of returning to "the Dewey archipelago," and remaining there for business and a career, show that Americans have the true colonizing spirit and, after a little experience, will equal the Dutch or English in ability and success.

Since the opening of this century we have obtained from Spain, France, Mexico, and Russia nearly four-fifths of the area of the present United States, that is, 2,700,375 square miles, of the total 3,501,000 of the United States before the war with Spain. We have had a century of experience in surveying, settling, developing, and governing large areas. Having had many nations within one nation, we have gained that long experience in dealing with large complex populations which forms the best warrant of our likelihood of ability to deal with the new populations in the Indies, both West and East.

Providence directing us, and laying large responsibilities upon us, but not too much at one time, has timed the call to new work and duties. This great work of governing West Indian mixed races, Hawaiians and Polynesians and Filipinos of varied ethnic stocks, has been given to us when we have been made measurably ready. The nation was never so completely solidified as at present, nor the Indians so quiet and easily managed as now. It is even probable that within a generation or two, having been fairly well civilized, they will be made citizens. The negroes have shown themselves responsive to opportunity. Some of the best regiments of our regulars are black. There is a still larger army of good teachers, preachers, business men, and skilled mechanics helping to fight ignorance and build up the country. In spite of occasional outbreaks, the success attained in governing the ignorant and turbulent European immigrants and the red and black people of our country, augurs well for our success in dealing with the Malays. There is little doubt but that the various new peoples, inhabiting the "Dewey archipelago," will respond to justice, kindness, and opportunity, even as the negro and the Indian have done.

The new acquisitions to the United States territory, whether as integral portions, colonies, or protectorate dependencies, that is, Porto Rico, Cuba, Hawaii, the Philippines, and other islands in the Pacific Ocean, over which our flag floats, make a total of about 170,000 square miles, or an area about as large as California with Massachusetts and Connecticut added on. This new population of from 10,000,000 to 12,000,000 makes the number of souls under the American flag not far from 90,000,000.

The whole trend of modern history seems to be toward colonization and protectorates of the more highly civilized among the less civilized nations; or, in other words, the mastery of the living over the dying nations. Heretofore the pagan and half-civilized nations were controlled from within their own borders, but during the last three or four centuries the nations possessing Christian civilization have overflowed from Europe into other continents, so that now nearly 500,000,000 people, once governed by themselves so far as they had any political order, are under the control of Christian governments.

The steps in succession, as we have traced them in the "Romance of Discovery" and the "Romance of American Colonization," seem to have been, — the work of Prince Henry the navigator in exploring the coast of Africa and beyond, Columbus's discovery of America, the Spanish and Portuguese colonies in the New World and in Asia, the Dutch explorations and conquests, the entrance of England as a leading colonizing power upon the scene, the American Revolution, and the expansion of Great Britain, until now we see under her control 9,000,000 square miles of the world's territory, and, besides nations that speak her tongue and look up to her as a mother, pupil nations in Asia and Africa by the score. We see Anglo-Saxon influence and ideas extending over the Dark Continent, in which a railway from the Mediterranean to the Cape of Good Hope is planned. Russia, dominating all northern Asia, owns 6,564,778, France 3,617,327, Germany 1,020,070, and the Netherlands 782,803 square miles, while Spain, Portugal, and Denmark have the remainder of the 22,288,153 square miles brought under European influences during four centuries. Over 8,000,000 in the nineteenth century before 1880, and nearly 9,000,000 square miles have been obtained between 1880 and 1898. Thus one-half the entire population of the globe is under the control of European governments. Of the 52,000,000 square miles of the whole world, over 22,000,000 square miles are held in a colonial or protectorate form. It has been impossible for the United States not to follow the drift of history. From her little narrow strip between the Alleghanies and the sea, she has grown to her present vast proportions.

This movement of the Aryan race seems to have been ordered by Him who bade Paul make his voyage from Asia, to introduce Christianity and democracy in Europe, who sent the Pilgrims in the *Mayflower* to America, and who despatched the missionary ship *Morning Star* to the Pacific islands, carrying out the ideas and the idealism of that democracy founded by Jesus, which is yet to fill the earth.

Yet despite the willingness of the American people to fight when necessary, and of the American youth to turn soldier when his country calls, the genius of our people is peaceful. There is little fear of militarism getting a grip upon us. General Grant, our greatest soldier, was also our true champion of peace, and successfully inaugurated arbitration on a large scale. President Arthur named our country the Great Pacific Power. President McKinley, accepting war only as the last resort, has shown himself a lover of peace more than of battle. At the Omaha Exposition in October, 1898, which was in itself a revelation of the rapid development of the trans-Mississippi region, he uttered the sentiment of the nation, — "We must follow duty, even if desire opposes." He with thoughtful Americans sees that a new era has opened for this republic, with new opportunities, new duties, new responsibilities, and necessarily new principles of initiative and new methods of action.

The triumphs of peace are greater than those of war. Though the clamor of the aggressively selfish is very noisy, yet the real heart of the American people is for peace. The conscience of the nation will urge our people to justice and generosity in dealing with the newer peoples under United States control. They will be willing to make sacrifices, in order to do for the islanders of the Pacific what they had done in times past for those within our own borders and beyond. American expansion is not one of territory only.

The romance of conquest is not that of triumph over enemies only. In the long and glorious story, we have learned to conquer ourselves. Our truest victories have been over slavery, dishonesty, bad money, duelling, lynch law, violence, drunkenness, and the liquor power. Progress often seems slow, and there remains yet a vast domain, to be yet wholly subdued, of sectionalism, violence, cruelty, and lawlessness. We have much ignorance and illiteracy to conquer, sectionalism and race hatreds to overcome, and the long inheritance of European feudalism to overmaster.

Nevertheless, with our material progress, moral reform has gone gloriously forward. As in national politics, the centrifugal forces of nullification and secession have been overcome, so in our day the centripetal or unifying forces have increased. By the solvent of the war with Spain, and in face of our new responsibilities, the sectionalisms of North and South, East and West, have been melted. The nation was never so strong in unity of spirit as to-day.

Our inventions have conquered space and time. One can go from San Francisco to Manila seven times in the same period which Marcus Whitman required to reach Washington from Oregon. We have conquered pain and disease, and lengthened life. Armed by the science of medicine and in the armor of correct hygiene, the white man can live safely and even comfortably in the tropics.

Our government has responded to the invitation of the Czar of Russia, who has proposed a congress of disarmament, which, if even partially carried out, may lead to the United States of Europe and the federation of the world — in both of which aims the Russian ruler was anticipated by William Penn, the founder of Pennsylvania, whose writings are to-day classics. The meeting is set for May 18, at the Hague, in the House in the Woods. Our American delegates are Ambassador Andrew D. White, one of the ablest American diplomatists, who has kept the peace with Germany; Seth Low, President of Columbia University; Captain William Crozier of the army, and Captain Alfred T. Mahan of the navy of the United States, and Stanford Newell, our minister to the Netherlands.

In the light of our history, the words of President McKinley, at Omaha, seem less impulsive optimism than sure prophecy, —

"The genius of the nation, its freedom, its wisdom, its humanity, its courage, its justice, favored by Divine Providence, will make it equal to every task and the master of every emergency."

A REVOLUTIONARY MAID. A Story of the Middle Period of the War for Independence. By AMY E. BLANCHARD. 321 pp. Cloth, $1.50.

The stirring times in and around New York following the pulling down of the statue of George the Third by the famous "Liberty Boys," brings to the surface the patriotism of the young heroine of the story. This act of the New York patriots obliged Kitty De Witt to decide whether she would be a Tory or a Revolutionary maid, and a patriot good and true she became. Her many and various experiences are very interestingly pictured, making this a happy companion book to "A Girl of '76."

*T*HE GOLDEN TALISMAN. By H. PHELPS WHITMARSH. 300 pp. Cloth, $1.50.

The narrative is based upon the adventures of a young Persian noble, who, being forced to leave his own country, leads an army against the mysterious mountain kingdom of Kaffirias. Though defeated and taken prisoner by the enemy, the hero's talisman saves his life and, later, leads him into kingly favor.

A valuable fund of information regarding the various plants, woods, and animals which furnish the world with perfume is happily interwoven into the story.

*W*HEAT AND HUCKLEBERRIES; Dr. Northmore's Daughters. By CHARLOTTE M. VAILE. 336 pp. Cloth, $1.50.

Mrs. Vaile has drawn the characters for her new book from the Middle West. But as the two girls spent their summer at their grandfather's in New England, a capital groundwork is furnished for giving the local color of both sections of the country. The story is bright and spirited and the two girls are sure to find their place among the favorite characters in fiction. All those who have read the Orcutt stories will welcome this new book by Mrs. Vaile.

*W*ITH PERRY ON LAKE ERIE. A Tale of 1812. By JAMES OTIS. 307 pp. Cloth, $1.50.

The story carries the reader from March until October of 1813, being laid on Lake Erie, detailing the work of the gallant Perry, who at the time of his famous naval victory was but twenty-seven years of age. From the time the keels of the vessels which became famous were laid until the victory was won which made Perry's name imperishable, the reader is kept in close touch with all that concerned Perry, and not only the main facts but the minor details of the story are historically correct.

Just the kind of historical story that young people — boys especially — are intensely interested in.

*B*ARBARA'S HERITAGE; or, Young Americans Among the Old Italian Masters. By D. L. HOYT. 325 pp. Cloth, $1.50.

We welcome a book from the pen of Miss Hoyt, whose foreign travel and study has made possible an exceedingly interesting story, into which has been interwoven much instructive and valuable information.

With a desire to broaden the education of her son and daughter by the opportunities afforded in foreign travel, an American mother takes them to Italy, and the author in a very happy strain has given us their many experiences. Replete with numerous illustrations and half-tones, it makes a handsome and attractive volume.

W. A. Wilde Company, Publishers.

T*HE QUEEN'S RANGERS.* By Charles Ledyard Norton. 352 pp. Cloth, $1.50.

The thrilling period during the last years of our struggle for independence forms the groundwork for Colonel Norton's latest work.

The intense patriotism which prompted our young men to do and dare anything for their country is shown in the exploits of the three young heroes.

By enlisting for a time beneath His Majesty's flag they were able to give much valuable information to the colonial cause.

With historical truth the author in this, his latest book, has happily coupled an exceedingly interesting and instructive story.

T*HE ROMANCE OF CONQUEST.* The Story of American Expansion through Arms and Diplomacy. By William E. Griffis. 312 pp. Cloth, $1.50.

In concise form it is the story of American expansion from the birth of the nation to the present day.

The reader will find details of every war. Anecdote enlivens the story from July 4, 1776, down to the days of Dewey, Sampson, and Schley, and of Miles, Merritt, Shafter, and Otis. It is a book as full of rapid movement as a novel.

W*HEN BOSTON BRAVED THE KING.* A Story of Tea-Party Times. By W. E. Barton, D. D. 314 pp. Cloth, $1.50.

One of the most absorbing stories of the Colonial-Revolutionary period published. The author is perfectly at home with his subject, and the story will be one of the popular books of the year.

"Though largely a story of boys and for boys, it has the liveliest interest for all classes of readers, and makes a strong addition to Dr. Barton's already notable series of historical tales."—*Christian Endeavor World.*

"It is a pleasure to read and to recommend such a book as this. In fact, we must say at the very beginning, that Dr. Barton is becoming one of the most skilful and enjoyable of American story-tellers."—*Boston Journal.*

C*ADET STANDISH OF THE ST. LOUIS.* A Story of Our Naval Campaign in Cuban Waters. By William Drysdale. 352 pp. Cloth, $1.50.

A strong, stirring story of brave deeds bravely done. A vivid picture of one of the most interesting and eventful periods of the late Spanish War.

"It is what the boys are likely to call 'a rattling good story.'"—*Cleveland Plain Dealer.*

"Mr. Drysdale has drawn an effective picture of the recent war with Spain in his new book. The story is full of dash and fire without being too sensational."—*Congregationalist.*

A *DAUGHTER OF THE WEST.* The Story of an American Princess. By Evelyn Raymond. 347 pp. Cloth, $1.50.

Interesting, wholesome, and admirable in every way is Mrs. Raymond's latest story for girls. Descriptions of California life are one of the fascinations of the book.

"A well-written story of Western life and adventure, which has for its heroine a brave, high-minded girl."—*Chronicle Telegraph, Pittsburg.*

"Laid among the broad valleys and lofty mountains of California every chapter is crowded full of most interesting experiences."—*Christian Endeavor World.*

W. A. Wilde Company, Boston and Chicago.

W. A. Wilde Company, Publishers.

War of the Revolution Series.
By Everett T. Tomlinson.

THREE COLONIAL BOYS. A Story of the Times of '76. 368 pp. Cloth, $1.50.

It is a story of three boys who were drawn into the events of the times, is patriotic, exciting, clean, and healthful, and instructs without appearing to. The heroes are manly boys, and no objectionable language or character is introduced. The lessons of courage and patriotism especially will be appreciated in this day. — *Boston Transcript.*

THREE YOUNG CONTINENTALS. A Story of the American Revolution. 364 pp. Cloth, $1.50.

This story is historically true. It is the best kind of a story either for boys or girls, and is an attractive method of teaching history.—*Journal of Education, Boston.*

WASHINGTON'S YOUNG AIDS. A Story of the New Jersey Campaign, 1776-1777. 391 pp. Cloth, $1.50.

The book has enough history and description to give value to the story which ought to captivate enterprising boys. — *Quarterly Book Review.*

The historical details of the story are taken from old records. These include accounts of the life on the prison ships and prison houses of New York, the raids of the pine robbers, the tempting of the Hessians, the end of Fagan and his band, etc. — *Publisher's Weekly.*

Few boys' stories of this class show so close a study of history combined with such genial story-telling power. — *The Outlook.*

TWO YOUNG PATRIOTS. A Story of Burgoyne's Invasion. 366 pp. Cloth, $1.50.

The crucial campaign in the American struggle for independence came in the summer of 1777, when Gen. John Burgoyne marched from Canada to cut the rebellious colonies asunder and join another British army which was to proceed up the valley of the Hudson. The American forces were brave, hard fighters, and they worried and harassed the British and finally defeated them. The history of this campaign is one of great interest and is well brought out in the part which the "two young patriots" took in the events which led up to the surrender of General Burgoyne and his army.

The set of four volumes in a box, $6.00.

SUCCESS. By ORISON SWETT MARDEN. Author of "Pushing to the Front," "Architects of Fate," etc. 317 pp. Cloth, $1.25.

It is doubtful whether any success books for the young have appeared in modern times which are so thoroughly packed from lid to lid with stimulating, uplifting, and inspiring material as the self-help books written by Orison Swett Marden. There is not a dry paragraph nor a single line of useless moralizing in any of his books.

To stimulate, inspire, and guide is the mission of his latest book, "Success," and helpfulness is its keynote. Its object is to spur the perplexed youth to act the Columbus to his own undiscovered possibilities; to urge him not to wait for great opportunities, but to seize common occasions and make them great, for he cannot tell when fate may take his measure for a higher place.

W. A. Wilde Company, Boston and Chicago.

W. A. Wilde Company, Publishers.

Brain and Brawn Series.
By William Drysdale.

THE YOUNG REPORTER. A Story of Printing House Square. 300 pp. Cloth, $1.50.

I commend the book unreservedly. — *Golden Rule.*
"The Young Reporter" is a rattling book for boys. — *New York Recorder.*
The best boys' book I ever read. — *Mr. Phillips, Critic for New York Times.*

THE FAST MAIL. A Story of a Train Boy. 328 pp. Cloth, $1.50.

"The Fast Mail" is one of the very best American books for boys brought out this season. Perhaps there could be no better confirmation of this assertion than the fact that the little sons of the present writer have greedily devoured the contents of the volume, and are anxious to know how soon they are to get a sequel. — *The Art Amateur, New York.*

THE BEACH PATROL. A Story of the Life-Saving Service. 318 pp. Cloth, $1.50.

The style of narrative is excellent, the lesson inculcated of the best, and, above all, the boys and girls are real. — *New York Times.*
A book of adventure and daring, which should delight as well as stimulate to higher ideals of life every boy who is so happy as to possess it. — *Examiner.*
It is a strong book for boys and young men. — *Buffalo Commercial.*

THE YOUNG SUPERCARGO. A Story of the Merchant Marine. 352 pp. Cloth, $1.50.

Kit Silburn is a real "Brain and Brawn" boy, full of sense and grit and sound good qualities. Determined to make his way in life, and with no influential friends to give him a start, he does a deal of hard work between the evening when he first meets the stanch Captain Griffith, and the proud day when he becomes purser of a great ocean steamship. His sea adventures are mostly on shore; but whether he is cleaning the cabin of the *North Cape*, or landing cargo in Yucatan, or hurrying the spongers and fruitmen of Nassau, or exploring London, or sight seeing with a disguised prince in Marseilles, he is always the same busy, thoroughgoing, manly Kit. Whether or not he has a father alive is a question of deep interest throughout the story; but that he has a loving and loyal sister is plain from the start.

The set of four volumes in a box, $6.00.

SERAPH, THE LITTLE VIOLINISTE. By Mrs. C. V. Jamieson. 300 pp. Cloth, $1.50.

The scene of the story is the French quarter of New Orleans, and charming bits of local color add to its attractiveness. — *The Boston Journal.*
Perhaps the most charming story she has ever written is that which describes Seraph, the little violiniste. — *Transcript, Boston.*

W. A. Wilde Company, Boston and Chicago.

Travel=Adventure Series.

IN WILD AFRICA. Adventures of Two Boys in the Sahara Desert, etc. By THOS. W. KNOX. 325 pp. Cloth, $1.50.

A story of absorbing interest. — *Boston Journal.*
Our young people will pronounce it unusually good. — *Albany Argus.*
Col. Knox has struck a popular note in his latest volume. — *Springfield Republican.*

THE LAND OF THE KANGAROO. By THOS. W. KNOX. Adventures of Two Boys in the Great Island Continent. 318 pp. Cloth, $1.50.

His descriptions of the natural history and botany of the country are very interesting. — *Detroit Free Press.*
The actual truthfulness of the book needs no gloss to add to its absorbing interest. — *The Book Buyer, New York.*

OVER THE ANDES; or, Our Boys in New South America. By HEZEKIAH BUTTERWORTH. 368 pp. Cloth, $1.50.

No writer of the present century has done more and better service than Hezekiah Butterworth in the production of helpful literature for the young. In this volume he writes, in his own fascinating way, of a country too little known by American readers. — *Christian Work.*

Mr. Butterworth is careful of his historic facts, and then he charmingly interweaves his quaint stories, legends, and patriotic adventures as few writers can. — *Chicago Inter-Ocean.*

The subject is an inspiring one, and Mr. Butterworth has done full justice to the high ideals which have inspired the men of South America. — *Religious Telescope.*

LOST IN NICARAGUA; or, The Lands of the Great Canal. By HEZEKIAH BUTTERWORTH. 295 pp. Cloth, $1.50.

The book pictures the wonderful land of Nicaragua and continues the story of the travelers whose adventures in South America are related in "Over the Andes." In this companion book to "Over the Andes," one of the boy travelers who goes into the Nicaraguan forests in search of a quetzal, or the royal bird of the Aztecs, falls into an ancient idol cave, and is rescued in a remarkable way by an old Mosquito Indian. The narrative is told in such a way as to give the ancient legends of Guatemala, the story of the chieftain, Nicaragua, the history of the Central American Republics, and the natural history of the wonderlands of the ocelot, the conger, parrots, and monkeys.

Since the voyage of the *Oregon*, of 13,000 miles to reach Key West the American people have seen what would be the value of the Nicaragua Canal. The book gives the history of the projects for the canal, and facts about Central America, and a part of it was written in Costa Rica. It enters a new field.

The set of four volumes in a box, $6.00.

QUARTERDECK AND FOK'SLE. By MOLLY ELLIOTT SEAWELL. 272 pp. Cloth, $1.25.

Miss Seawell has done a notable work for the young people of our country in her excellent stories of naval exploits. They are of the kind that causes the reader, no matter whether young or old, to thrill with pride and patriotism at the deeds of daring of the heroes of our navy.

Fighting for the Flag Series.

By Chas. Ledyard Norton.

JACK BENSON'S LOG; or, Afloat with the Flag in '61. 281 pp. Cloth, $1.25.

An unusually interesting historical story, and one that will arouse the loyal impulses of every American boy and girl. The story is distinctly superior to anything ever attempted along this line before. — *The Independent.*
A story that will arouse the loyal impulses of every American boy and girl. — *The Press.*

A MEDAL OF HONOR MAN; or, Cruising Among Blockade Runners. 280 pp. Cloth, $1.25.

A bright, breezy sequel to "Jack Benson's Log." The book has unusual literary excellence. — *The Book Buyer, New York.*
A stirring story for boys. — *The Journal, Indianapolis.*

MIDSHIPMAN JACK. 290 pp. Cloth, $1.25.

Jack is a delightful hero, and the author has made his experiences and adventures seem very real. — *Congregationalist.*
It is true historically and full of exciting war scenes and adventures. — *Outlook.*
A stirring story of naval service in the Confederate waters during the late war. — *Presbyterian.*

The set of three volumes in a box, $3.75.

A GIRL OF '76. BY AMY E. BLANCHARD. 331 pp. Cloth, $1.50.

"A Girl of '76" lays its scene in and around Boston where the principal events of the early period of the Revolution were enacted. Elizabeth Hall, the heroine, is the daughter of a patriot who is active in the defense of his country. The story opens with a scene in Charlestown, where Elizabeth Hall and her parents live. The emptying of the tea in Boston Harbor is the means of giving the little girl her first strong impression as to the seriousness of her father's opinions, and causes a quarrel between herself and her schoolmate and playfellow, Amos Dwight.

A SOLDIER OF THE LEGION. BY CHAS. LEDYARD NORTON. 300 pp. Cloth, $1.50.

Two boys, a Carolinian and a Virginian, born a few years apart during the last half of the eighteenth century, afford the groundwork for the incidents of this tale.
The younger of the two was William Henry Harrison, sometime President of the United States, and the elder, his companion and faithful attendant through life, was Carolinus Bassett, Sergeant of the old First Infantry, and in an irregular sort of a way Captain of Virginian Horse. He it is who tells the story a few years after President Harrison's death, his granddaughter acting as critic and amanuensis.
The story has to do with the early days of the Republic, when the great, wild, unknown West was beset by dangers on every hand, and the Government at Washington was at its wits' end to provide ways and means to meet the perplexing problems of national existence.

W. A. Wilde Company, Boston and Chicago.

THE ORCUTT GIRLS; or, One Term at the Academy. By CHARLOTTE M. VAILE. 316 pp. Cloth, $1.50.

A well-told story of school life which will interest its readers deeply, and hold before them a high standard of living. The heroines are charming girls and their adventures are described in an entertaining way. — *Pilgrim Teacher.*

Mrs. Vaile gives us a story here which will become famous as a description of a phase of New England educational history which has now become a thing of the past, with an exception here and there. — *Boston Transcript.*

SUE ORCUTT. A Sequel to "The Orcutt Girls." By CHARLOTTE M. VAILE. 330 pp. Cloth, $1.50.

It is a charming story from beginning to end and is written in that easy flowing style which characterizes the best stories of our best writers. — *Christian Work.*

It is wholly a piece of good fortune for young folks that brings this book to market in such ample season for the selection of holiday gifts. — *Denver Republican.*

The story teaches a good moral without any preaching, in fact it is as good in a way as Miss Alcott's books, which is high but deserved praise. — *Chronicle.*

THE M. M. C. A Story of the Great Rockies. By CHARLOTTE M. VAILE. 232 pp. Cloth, $1.25.

The pluck of the little school teacher, struggling against adverse circumstances, to hold for her friend the promising claim, which he has secured after years of misfortune in other ventures, is well brought out. The almost resistless bad luck which has made "Old Hopefull's" nickname a hollow mockery still followed him when a fortune was almost within his grasp. The little school teacher was, however, a new element in "Old Hopefull's" experience, and the result, as the story shows, was most satisfactory.

THE ROMANCE OF DISCOVERY; or, a Thousand Years of Exploration, etc. By WILLIAM ELLIOT GRIFFIS. 305 pp. Cloth, $1.50.

It is a book of profit and interest involving a variety of correlated instances and influences which impart the flavor of the unexpected. — *Philadelphia Presbyterian.*

An intensely interesting narrative following well-authenticated history. — *Telescope.*

Boys will read it for the romance in it and be delighted, and when they get through, behold! they have read a history of America. — *Awakener.*

THE ROMANCE OF AMERICAN COLONIZATION; or, How the Foundations of Our Country Were Laid. By WILLIAM ELLIOT GRIFFIS. 295 pp. Cloth, $1.50.

To this continent, across a great ocean, came two distinct streams of humanity and two rival civilizations, — the one Latin, led and typified by the Spanish, with Portugese and French also, and the other Germanic, or Anglo-Saxon, led and typified by the English and reinforced by Dutch, German, and British people.

A SON OF THE REVOLUTION. An Historical Novel of the Days of Aaron Burr. By ELBRIDGE S. BROOKS. 301 pp. Cloth, $1.50.

The story of Tom Edwards, adventurer, as it is connected with Aaron Burr, is in every way faithful to the facts of history. As the story progresses the reader will wonder where the line between fact and fiction is to be drawn. Among the characters that figure in it are President Jefferson, Gen. Andrew Jackson, General Wilkinson, and many other prominent government and army officials.

W. A. Wilde Company, Boston and Chicago.

MALVERN, A NEIGHBORHOOD STORY. By Ellen Douglas Deland. 341 pp. Cloth, $1.50.

Her descriptions of boys and girls are so true, and her knowledge of their ways is so accurate, that one must feel an admiration for her complete mastery of her chosen field. — *The Argus, Albany.*

Miss Deland was accorded a place with Louisa M. Alcott and Nora Perry as a successful writer of books for girls. We think this praise none too high. — *The Post.*

A SUCCESSFUL VENTURE. By Ellen Douglas Deland. 340 pp. Cloth, $1.50.

One of the many successful books that have come from her pen, which is certainly the very best. — *Boston Herald.*

It is a good piece of work and its blending of good sense and entertainment will be appreciated. — *Congregationalist.*

KATRINA. By Ellen Douglas Deland. 340 pp. Cloth, $1.50.

"Katrina" is the story of a girl who was brought up by an aunt in a remote village of Vermont. Her life is somewhat lonely until a family from New York come there to board during the summer. Katrina's aunt, who is a reserved woman, has told her little of her antecedents, and she supposes that she has no other relatives. Her New York friends grow very fond of her and finally persuade her to visit them during the winter. There new pleasures and new temptations present themselves, and Katrina's character develops through them to new strength.

ABOVE THE RANGE. By Theodora R. Jenness. 332 pp. Cloth, $1.25.

The quaintness of the characters described will be sure to make the story very popular. — *Book News, Philadelphia.*

A book of much interest and novelty. — *The Book Buyer, New York.*

BIG CYPRESS. By Kirk Munroe. 164 pp. Cloth, $1.00.

If there is a man who understands writing a story for boys better than another, it is Kirk Munroe. — *Springfield Republican.*

A capital writer of boys' stories is Mr. Kirk Munroe. — *Outlook.*

FOREMAN JENNIE. By Amos R. Wells. A Young Woman of Business. 268 pp. Cloth, $1.25.

It is a delightful story. — *The Advance, Chicago.*
It is full of action. — *The Standard, Chicago.*
A story of decided merit. — *The Epworth Herald, Chicago.*

MYSTERIOUS VOYAGE OF THE DAPHNE. By Lieut. H. P. Whitmarsh. 305 pp. Cloth, $1.25.

One of the best collections of short stories for boys and girls that has been published in recent years. Such writers as Hezekiah Butterworth, Wm. O. Stoddard, and Jane G. Austin have contributed characteristic stories which add greatly to the general interest of the book.

W. A. Wilde Company, Boston and Chicago.

www.ingramcontent.com/pod-product-compliance
Lightning Source LLC
Chambersburg PA
CBHW030013240426

43672CB00007B/933